Contents List

Finding and Collecting

Collecting
**Flowers and
Leaves
Stamps**

Tracking
**Stones
Towns and
Countries
Coins**

Collecting

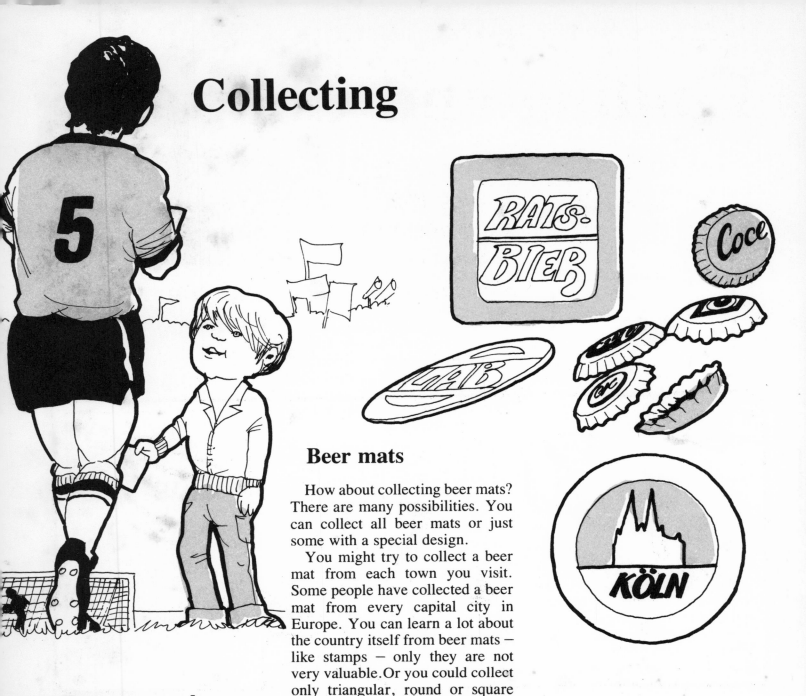

Famous people

Many people, young and old, enjoy collecting things. Some collect art treasures, others collect stones. There have been well-known collectors of toy cars, and others who collect people — famous people.

No, not the people themselves but their autographs. You all know what an autograph is, don't you? When a famous personality comes to town people queue up to get an autograph, a signature.

If you want to collect famous signatures perhaps you could choose a special subject: autographs of pop stars, politicians, football players or other sporting people. It makes it much easier to complete a collection.

Beer mats

How about collecting beer mats? There are many possibilities. You can collect all beer mats or just some with a special design.

You might try to collect a beer mat from each town you visit. Some people have collected a beer mat from every capital city in Europe. You can learn a lot about the country itself from beer mats — like stamps — only they are not very valuable. Or you could collect only triangular, round or square mats. Ask your parents to help you to collect these from pubs or hotels they visit.

Other people collect different bottle tops from drink bottles.

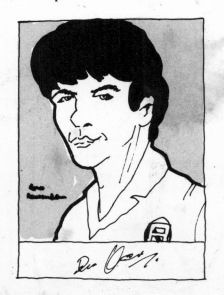

Boxes

Some people collect boxes. There are wooden boxes with intricate carvings, ivory boxes from India, 200-year-old hairgrip boxes and mysterious jewellery boxes with secret compartments.

Have you ever noticed how pretty some cheese boxes look? Especially the camembert boxes from France which show a variety of different pictures and tell a little about the area where the cheese was from.

For a time, the collecting of matchboxes was very popular. There are the usual household matches, then the ones with advertising on them. Matchboxes

from Italy are especially pretty as they are usually printed with pictures of animals, flowers or monuments.

Many of these boxes are made from plastic nowadays. Why don't you start collecting wooden boxes? You never know, they might become valuable some day when there aren't any wooden ones around anymore.

On this page you'll find a wide range of different ideas for collecting things. You'll probably recognise them all.

Walking along the road you can see one of the greatest collecting passions for many people: collecting car stickers. Some cars are almost covered with stickers from countries and places the car has been taken to. Bicycles and motorbikes, too, are often 'decorated' in this way.

But there aren't just stickers of countries, towns or places of interest. Some stickers have jokes or slogans, and some have a message for other drivers. Parents with young children sometimes attach a sticker to their car: 'Baby on Board'! They want to make other drivers take more care when driving behind them.

You could also collect sugar cubes or sachets from cafés and restaurants. Some show the name of the place, and these can be a good reminder of your visit.

Ornaments are things which nobody really needs. But just make a point of noticing how many houses are crammed full with ornaments. They could be small animals, stones, toys and other things. Spare buttons are not only useful to keep to replace those lost from your clothes. A colourful collection of buttons is a super thing. Or you could collect old keys and cover a wall with them. Can you think of other things to collect?

Take nature home with you

In the spring, summer and autumn our world is still very beautiful. But that is not so noticeable in the cities any more. Parks are just for people who want to walk about in their Sunday best. They can be rather boring.

So let's get out into the country. By bicycle, bus or car — take the whole family! Go for walks, look at nature, breathe it in, and take a little home with you.

Collect leaves and flowers which you can press at home and arrange in order. Only pick flowers where there are plenty and don't pull them out with their roots. Only take single leaves and not the entire branch. Or wait until autumn when the leaves fall down of their own accord.

How to press flowers and leaves

Place the flowers or leaves between two sheets of blotting paper and weigh them down with heavy books. Leave them there for about a week.

Try to keep the original shape. Press cup-shaped flowers on their sides, for example. Roses should be opened up and pressed from the front.

How to keep flowers and leaves

Drying

Some flowers are very good for drying; you have to find out which. Leave long stems when picking. Tie stems together and hang them upside down.

Preserving

Mix two parts of warm water with one part of glycerine (from chemists). Leave the mixture to cool down. Cut off the flowers you wish to preserve as near to the root as possible, peel off a little from the stem and split the end. Submerge the flowers into the liquid and leave for three days. Flowers with fleshy leaves and petals last much longer.

Printing

Leaves are very good for this. Paint the leaves with watercolours and quickly press the painted side onto paper. (See, also, the chapter about printing on page 110.)

Transfers

The shapes of flowers and leaves can also be traced on transfer paper. You will get the main shape and can fill in the detailed structures afterwards to transfer interesting patterns.

Your nature collection could look like this:

Take a ring binder with a new refill. Stick flowers and leaves on the empty pages. Arrange them according to the name of the printed leaves or transferred flowers and leaves.

You could also arrange your collection according to the seasons: In the spring snowdrops then celandines are in flower; in summer buttercups and daisies; in the autumn and winter there are many interesting grasses, ferns and leaves.

Or place them in alphabetical order: Under A would be Aaron's rod, anemone or apple tree leaf.

Another possibility would be to collect a flower or plant for each letter. You could note anything you know about the flowers or leaves and where you found them.

You could also arrange your flower and leaf collection according to season. You can take single flowers or a whole bunch to stick in your album.

What else you can do with flowers and leaves

Friends and relatives are always pleased with home-made presents. Why don't you send your aunt a nice flower card for her next birthday? (Also see the section on collage on page 116.) You could make a picture from flowers and leaves, perhaps a bird as on our illustration, or a tree, your garden, a head or children playing.

Surprise your mother with a flower necklace. Make a calendar arranging the leaves and flowers to match the months they are in season. Even lampshades can be stuck with flowers and leaves.

A flower doll

To begin with you need four dry sticks for the skeleton of your flower doll. Tie the sticks together as shown in figure 1, adding a little glue if necessary. To make the doll stand up you will need a third leg for support.

Now cut out thin strips of cardboard and use to form the body and dress as shown in figure 2. The head is formed from the dried seed pod of a flower. Stick on a few petals for hair. Paint the head with water colours.

To dress your doll, use dried or pressed flowers and leaves, and your imagination.

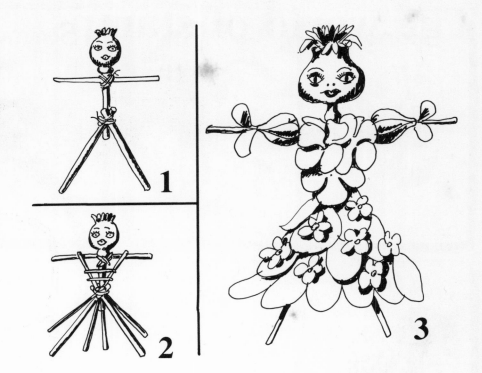

Miracles with flowers

Plants produce starch with the help of sunlight by way of 'photosynthesis'. You can use this process for your own plant miracle.

First cut out a piece of black paper in the shape of a leaf and fasten it to a leaf with a paperclip. Leave the leaf covered with the paper for a few days, then cut out a cross or another shape from the black paper.

Now leave the leaf for a few more days making sure that the side with the cross is pointing to the light. Mix a little iodine with water and brush it over the leaf. The area not previously covered with paper

will turn blue because of the production of starch — and you will have made a leaf with a blue cross.

Another miracle: Take a white carnation and carefully split it up the stem to the head. Now place one of the stem halves in a glass with blue tinted water, the other in a glass with red water. Within a short time the colour will move into the petals and you will have a two-coloured flower.

The world of stamps

Ever since stamps were invented they have been collected. That's understandable as stamps are among the most interesting things one can collect. But more about that later.

A clever person thought that it was much easier to raise the fee of transporting letters by sticking a stamp on them. The first self-sticking stamp was the 'Penny Black' in 1840 which was produced in England.

Today, stamps are printed all over the world to pay for postal

fees. But there are also stamps that are printed mainly for the stamp collector. For instance, there are many special stamps from San Marino, the tiny state in Italy.

Why are stamps sometimes worth so much? You might have heard of the 'Blue Mauritius', the most valuable stamp in the world. Generally, the more rare a thing is the more valuable it is. For example, if there is a bad world coffee harvest and there isn't much coffee available, then the price goes up. It is a bit like that with stamps. The 'Blue Mauritius' is the most valuable stamp because it is the rarest.

Over 5,000 new stamps are brought into postal circulation every year — quite a lot for the collector who wants to complete

his collection. That's why it might be more sensible to set yourself a less ambitious goal.

Making a start/ collecting stamps

If you want to start a stamp collection firstly tell all your friends, acquaintances and family about your plan. Perhaps somebody will give you their old collection because they've lost interest in it. Or you might be given a lot of old envelopes.

Start off in a small way. Cut out all the stamps from letters and postcards. Postcards from holiday destinations like Spain, Italy, Greece and Yugoslavia are not so rare nowadays, so your collection could soon grow.

Of course, you can always buy stamps from stamp shops or other collectors. But that can be too expensive.

The tools of the collector

Tweezers

Stamps should always be handled with a pair of tweezers as they can be damaged very easily. And when just one bit of the perforation is gone the stamp has lost any value.

Gummed strips

You can stick your stamps into your album and take them out again by using the gummed strip without damaging the stamp itself.

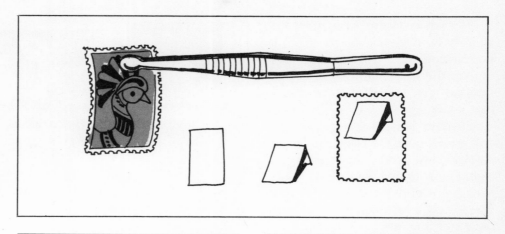

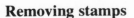

Removing stamps

Cut out the piece of the envelope or postcard where the stamp is attached with a pair of scissors. Place it in a saucer of warm water and leave it to soak. After a while most stamps will come off by themselves, otherwise carefully use tweezers. Place the stamps between two sheets of blotting paper to dry. Then they are ready to be arranged in your album.

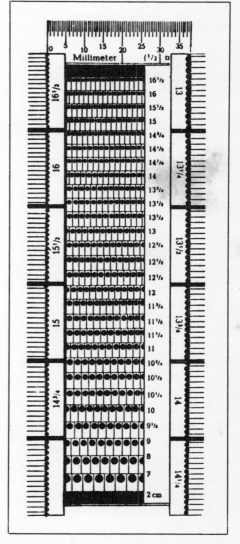

Stamp album

You can buy yourself an album, they are not too expensive. Or you could use a ring binder, or make an album from a cardboard carton, covering it with paper and film.

Perforation gauge

With this gauge and a stamp catalogue you can name and place even the most unusual stamp.

Suggestions to start with

At first select a country whose stamps you want to collect. You have to consider whether you can obtain stamps from that country. It might be difficult to collect just stamps from Tanzania or Zimbabwe. It might be more appropriate to collect from Great Britain, say, or from the Commonwealth. Or you might take a country from the Common Market. Or a favourite holiday country from which you might receive stamps more regularly.

To collect the stamps of an entire continent you might collect them according to the initial letter of the country or their geographical position from north to south; there are several ways.

Don't write the names of the countries directly into the album while your collection is still growing. Write them on little cards which you can change according to how many stamps you have of one country.

Quite a different way is to collect stamps according to motif. Each country has its own different motif which can tell a lot about the country itself, its history and regions, the people, animals and plants.

Brief guide to stamp collecting

There are used and unused stamps. The unused stamps are usually more valuable. They are the ones that haven't been on a letter at all. But there are some exceptions.

If letters or cards are marked with a special postmark they can be valuable, too. In that case leave the stamp on the envelope and collect these in a separate part of your album. Special postmarks are

given to commemorate certain dates, occasions or special sporting events like the football World Cup or the Olympic Games.

A complete set of stamps is of extra value. A set is all the stamps of a series with all the different denominations (prices). Some people collect entire blocks of stamps. These are sheets of ten by twenty stamps of the same value.

First day covers present a special interest for the collector. On these are the stamps of a special issue set complete with a special postmark for the first day of issue.

There are also stamps that have no perforations at all. These are called 'cut'.

To exchange means to learn

By exchanging stamps you can increase your collection. In addition you can exchange tips with other collectors and learn from them. Or you can learn through the motifs of your new stamps. It is a good idea to keep a special exchange album for stamps that either don't fit in your collection or you already have. And, of course, you can become a member of a stamp collectors' club where stamps are exchanged regularly and information is given about new issues.

Tracking

Tracks are signs. The prints of feet, claws, paws or tyres can all be seen on the ground. You can tell a lot by these tracks. The greater the body weight of the moving creature the clearer the print it will leave. Therefore the chains of a tank can be seen as prints on the surface of a road. Of course, the tracks of a rabbit won't show up on a road. You can see these on loose ground, and you can learn a lot about an animal's habits from its tracks. If a rabbit is fleeing from danger it will make a very different track from when it is hopping about merrily.

COW

HORSE

CAT

DOG

RABBIT

MARTEN

SQUIRREL

FOX

DEER

Animal tracks

Observing animal tracks you'll soon notice the main differences. You can tell immediately whether the animal had hooves, like a horse or a cow, or if it had soft paws like a rabbit, cat or dog. We don't need to tell you about the difference between bird and mammal tracks. To introduce you to the art of track-reading we have given the names of animals and their respective tracks in our illustration.

But tracks are left in quite another way, too, by animals. Feathers, bones or even their excrement gives information about the kind of animal. A good tracker can distinguish easily between the feather of a goose and one of a partridge.

Tracking signs

There are situations where it might be important to use signs. If you are in the woods with your friends, for example, and you want to let them know about something you can use tracking signs.

Here the apparent disorder in the woods or on the paths is an advantage. Thus a tree, a pile of stones of a few bent twigs that no one else would notice can be a clear sign to someone in the know.

As an introduction for the future tracker you'll find here a small guide to the most important tracking signs. Looking at some of the signs you may think we are a bit mad. But no, it could be important in some circumstances to lay wrong or misleading signs.

Human tracks

You know now about different kinds of tracks. But what, if the ground is covered with grass? Tracks on grass are rather difficult to see, so it is harder to identify what, or who made them, but you can still make some observations. If the grass is down-trodden you can tell by the direction the grass blades are bent which way the person went. In the woods you can tell the direction somebody went by the broken or bent twigs. If the track crosses a path or stream the direction of the track can be followed here, too, from wet or muddy footmarks.

But tracks in sand or loose soil are very easy to detect. On the illustration you see the prints of different people.

You see, the footprints of people can tell us quite a lot. Cowboy boots, the mocassins of Red Indians, the print of bare feet, a mother and child, football boots and running shoes with spikes will all make quite different tracks which will tell you something about the person who made them.

Paperchase

Paperchase is an exciting game. It is usually played with two groups of children. Two children are chosen or draw lots to form the group of track-setters. The others make up the group of followers. Now you must select the signs that are allowed. Among them, of course, should be some signs that are misleading. Then the two track-setters have a head-start of 15 minutes. They set off and lay the track for the followers— but using only the agreed signs.

After quarter of an hour the followers start off. They keep a look out for tracks as they run through the woods. If a sign has been spotted, all must agree on its meaning. If there are several interpretations the group has to split. but not forgetting to agree a time and place to meet up again. They must try to find and interpret the signs quickly so the advantage between the track-setters and followers becomes smaller and smaller until they have caught up with them.

If the track-setters are too clever to be caught they'll lay the sign for the 'end of track' at some point, hide themselves and laugh at the followers that crawl about on hands and knees looking for them.

This game can be altered in a variety of ways. Here are some suggestions:

A papaerchase can also be held in a village or town. But you must take into account that the signs there might inadvertently be changed or disturbed by other people. Therefore you should agree on signs that are not changeable.

The name of this game is derived from the way the inventors of it used to use scraps of paper to set the track. But you can use other things as well, like wood chips (taking care they don't blow away), markings in the sand, stones or plants.

Finally a tip for the track-setters: if you tramp about the ground so much that the followers just need to follow your footprints don't be surprised if they catch up with you in no time!

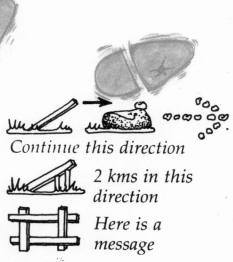

Continue this direction

2 kms in this direction

Here is a message

Attention, Danger

End of track

Wrong way, go back

Left or right

Right is wrong

Tree marker for direction

Greetings from the little stone men

Colorado in the United States of America and Almeria in Spain are stony deserts with canyons and rocks where famous Westerns (Cowboy films) are made. Nothing else can be done in these dead areas, unless you are out to catch a vulture, or collect stones.

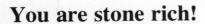

You are stone rich!

Collecting stones has indisputable advantages; it doesn't cost any money, so everybody can be stone rich if they want to be. And you won't become a stay-at-home either as it's quite impossible to collect stones sitting in front of the television. You really do have to get out into nature.

I want to tell you the story of Otto Klages. This old man found his first fossil when he was seven years old. Living in the town of Konigslutter, in Germany, which has the ideal conditions for a budding stone collector, as in this area fossils can be found from almost all geological ages.

He collected stones, first around the area near his home, then all over Germany, later in Europe and finally all over the world. Today he is one of the most famous experts in his field. For example, he found sea lilies (flower-shaped animals) which are over 200 million years old.

Otto Klages has given more than 20,000 fossils to museums and has founded fossil museums of his own. That needn't necessarily be your aim, but collecting stones is a fascinating hobby for everyone.

There are as many stony beaches as there are sandy beaches by the sea. Every stream carries pebbles, and fossils can be found almost anywhere. Fossils are stones which show the prints of plants and animals from millions of years ago. So you see, it is quite worthwhile to collect stones. You'll learn a lot about the formation of life, your environment and the earth at large.

Little stone men

There are also people that can turn stones into something else: stone men, for example. You only need a pile of stones or pebbles of different size and shape. These are put together to make a figure; they can be funny or have a special meaning.

Paint the stones with poster paints and lacquer them with clear varnish, but only very thinly as they shouldn't be too shiny. Then stick them together with strong adhesive in the shape you have in mind.

Town, country, river, plant, animal

Do you know this game? A letter of the alphabet is agreed upon and everybody has to write down quickly a town, a country, an animal etc. beginning with the same letter. Whoever finishes first wins. Points are given for each word — 10 for each, 5 if somebody else has the same, 20 if nobody else found one.

But here is another suggestion in connection with towns, countries and even continents — collect them!

My town

Here are some ideas, examples and suggestions for the various subjects connected with 'my town', but that doesn't mean that you have to keep to them. You might have much better ideas, more imagination and better inventive powers, so why not use them?

To start with I would get hold of a town map. My son, Andreas, lives in Aachen (Germany). So in his room there is a map of Aachen on the wall. He asks himself: what is unique to Aachen, different to other towns?

And he remembers: there is a beautiful old cathedral here. Aachen is famous for horse-riding events. Aachen lies at the borders of two countries, Belgium and Holland. Aachen has a large fair.

That's important for Andreas as this is not only a trade fair but also a fun fair where he likes to go on the roundabouts. But other things are important to him, too; his home, his school, the area where he goes to play, and the swimming pool. And the roads where his grandparents live (where he might sometimes get a little pocket money). Or the garden of one of the grandmas . . .

Andreas collects photographs, postcards, tickets, anything that he can find out about the things that interest him in Aachen. He sticks them around his map and connects them by string and pins to his favourite spots on the map. Now Andreas can quickly explain to visitors what he's been doing during the day, which routes he took and why he likes his home town so much.

name . . .

My county

You can do the same with a map of your county. But you could also draw such a map onto your wall — or on a large piece of paper. Now your relatives, friends and acquaintances are roped in to keep their eyes open and bring you anything that relates to the towns, villages, woods, lakes and reservoirs of your county. That can be postcards, photographs, cards, beer mats, advertisements, rare plants and stones, in short anything that belongs to the county where you live.

My country

If you are British you most probably live in Britain. You could collect anything connected with Britain, or another country you or your family have lived in, or are interested in. Or you could make comparisons and collect things from both countries.

You could, for example, concentrate on the big cities in Britain: Birmingham, Bristol, Cardiff, Edinburgh, Glasgow, London, Liverpool, Manchester, Newcastle and Southampton. Find out all you can about them and compare them with the big cities in the other country you are interested in.

You could collect posters of the various cities. But whether they will all fit on your wall is another problem. You'll need permission before you start decorating the whole house!

The countries of Europe

You need only walk along the streets of any major city and you'll soon be aware of foreign products everywhere. Notice the brands of cars, radios and televisions. Take a look at food wrappers, labels in shoes and shirts — they're full of German, Italian, French, Spanish and Greek names and terms. You'll often find a foreign name on bottles of drink and on many restaurants: A lot of these names come from Europe. And we are often visitors to Europe. At holiday times the ports and airports are packed with holidaymakers on their way to other European countries.

If you want to collect as much from European countries as possible, take a ring binder and start by inserting 12 sheets of paper. On each sheet, in alphabetical order, neatly trace the outline of one of the countries of Europe and write the name beside it.

These are the 'fly-leaves'. Behind these file everything you can find about the countries. You can become the proud owner of postcards from Yugoslavia, stamps from Greece, beer mats and photos from Spain. You can remove the labels from bottles and tins (soaking them off with water

The whole wide world

When looking at magazines you often find pictures of non-European countries and cities, exotic areas and strange peoples. If you can't yet fly across the great oceans to far away countries yourself, travel brochures can bring the world into your home.

You can collect things from these places, too. If you live near a port you'll have plenty of sources, and the same if your home is near an airport. If one of your relatives goes to, say, Honolulu make him promise to bring you back something typical of the country. When he gives it to you, get him to tell you everything about the place. You can write it all down. You can also get a lot of information about every country in the world from geography books and encyclopedias.

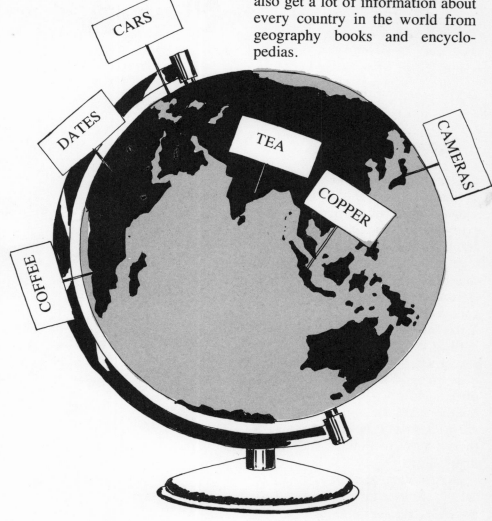

then allowing them to dry) and stick them in your book. You could have a 100-peseta note from Spain and matches from France, a bag of tulip bulbs from Holland, and from Belgium . . .! You could expand your collection and incorporate the USSR, Turkey, Bulgaria, San Marino and Monaco. You will get to know quite a lot about the various European countries.

Do you know the capitals of Europe?

The names of all the European countries are listed. Beside them is a space where you can write the capital city of the respective country. Can you do it all by yourself or do you need help? ·

Norway
Finland
Sweden
Denmark
Iceland
Ireland
Germany
Netherlands

Belgium
Luxembourg
Liechtenstein
Andorra
France
Spain
Portugal
Italy
Yugoslavia
Albania
Malta

Greece
Bulgaria
Rumania
Hungary
Czechoslovakia
USSR
Austria
Switzerland
Poland
Monaco
San Marino

Coins of the realm

Coins are pieces of money made from metal and embossed with an imprint. The first currencies were coins, and they have proved their worth until today. Coins are found in every country of the world.

Coins are much more than simply money. How could you get sweets from a vending machine if there weren't any coins for them? These round or angular pieces of metal can tell us about our history. On old coins you can see the faces of former kings. And today all British coins are embossed with the head of the Queen.

On the British £1 coin, on the reverse side of the Queen's head, you will see one of four designs. Representing England, the lion and the unicorn; representing Ireland, the flax plant; representing Scotland, the thistle, and representing Wales, the leek.

The prepared pieces of metal are pressed against a mould with great force and thus embossed. Coins are often minted for special occasions; the Commonwealth Games for example.

A complete set is more valuable

If you want to collect coins it is best to choose a particular sort. You can collect old coins to find out more about history. Or you could collect coins from European countries. It might be more difficult with far away countries if no one you know ever goes there!

But you could also try to complete a collection of all the coins of your own country. For this you must look very closely at any coin. You'll notice that they are all stamped with the year they were minted. Only when you have a complete set will the value go up. Try it! And if it doesn't work you will, at least, have saved something!

About the yen, lira, franc and mark

Every country has its own currency. When you go abroad you can change your own money into the currency of the country you're visiting. It wouldn't do to be without any money while you're on holiday!

Here is a small list of countries and their currencies. Try to complete the list, if you can.

Egypt – pound
Canada – Canadian dollar
Japan – yen
Belgium – Belgian franc
FDR – Deutsch mark
GDR – mark
Denmark – crown

France:
Italy:
Ireland:
Spain:
Portugal:
Sweden:
USA:
USSR:

Fun and Games

Bicycle
Ice skates
Roller skates
Skateboard
Calculator

Music
Instruments
Music tricks
    and technology
Camps and
    castles

Champions go fast — and safe

Before you get on your bicycle and ride off, do a check. Are the brakes, tyre pressures and lights OK? If not put them in order before you set out. Riders of unserviced bikes endanger themselves and others!

Now, let's start. Racing, of course, is most fun. There are various ways which will be described later. But, to be fair, make sure you all have the same odds — all use the same gear, for instance.

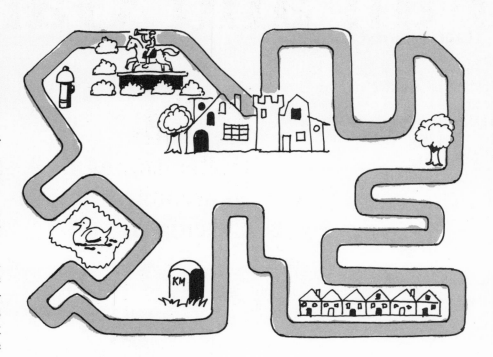

Why not start with a race in reverse? A snail-pace race. The winner is the one who comes last — the one who can stay still on his bike the longest. Take care to mark the track clearly or you might have a disaster.

And another tip: try to use quiet side roads, squares or parks for your races, relays and skill tests. Its too dangerous in road traffic.

Le-Mans-start

It's great fun to do a Le-Mans-Start. Park your bikes and mark the finishing line. At a sign from the starter you all line up in a row about 20 metres away from the bikes. The second sign is: 'On your bike', and you all run to your bikes. The one to pedal off first can get a good headstart, and the others must work hard to have a chance of winning the race. Mark your start and finish clearly or you might end up arguing!

Bike relay

In bike relay, several teams are involved. Divide yourselves up into two or more teams with equal numbers of bikes. Each team divides into two even-sized groups, positioned at either end of the track. The starters each hold a relay stick and race to the end of the track, where they hand the sticks to their team mates. The first complete team to finish racing is the winner. Take care not to drop the stick.

Rally aces

A great bike rally is taking place today! It has been prepared by two or three of you who won't take part, but will watch the rally and act as judges.

What you have prepared: a route across the town, woods or village, containing various parts and tasks like 'How many steps are there from the road to St. Mary's church?' 'What is the square with the town hall called?' 'How many trees are there in X-street?' 'What colour is the awning of the chemist's?' etc. (You can ask an adult for advice so as not to make any errors.)

Post invitations in your neighbourhood. The start-off is soon!

Now you collect a small entry fee from each participant to pay for the prizes.

Ready, steady go! Each mistake carries a time penalty of 10 seconds, so who is the winner?

Race against the time

This is a very simple way of holding an exciting race. All you need is four boxes or large tins and a stop-watch. You mark the top left hand box with the start and finish line:

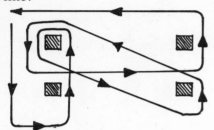

Stage 1: The round trip
The aim is to circle the top box twice and the others once each following the arrow.

Stage 2: The big eight
This stage is easy as you just drive a figure of eight around the boxes.

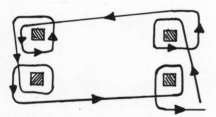

Stage 3: Looping
Each box must be looped once before the next box is taken on, from the outside.

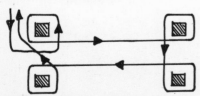

Stage 4: The inner course
The same as in stage 3 but the boxes must be circled from the inside and the finishing line must be crossed.

Add up the four times of each rider. Who is the fastest overall?

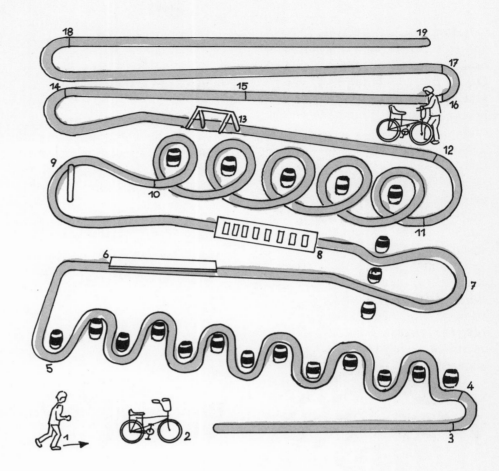

Obstacle course

An obstacle course is great fun. The winner is not necessarily the strongest contender — you have to be skillful, too.

Look at the drawing where we have devised a course with plenty of obstacles. But there are no limits to your own imagination. You could include waterways, cross-country courses or stretches where the bike has to be carried — there are countless possibilities.

Each participant starts on his own. The time is taken with a stop-watch. A well-ridden obstacle is applauded, a mistake receives a time penalty (work out your own system).

Each rider is cheered to spur him along. (If he's closely watched he can't cheat!) Each mistake is noted along with the finishing time for each rider. Mistakes are converted into seconds which are deducted from the finishing time. The clear winner is the rider with the shortest overall time.

Test for technical and artistic skill

Finally a few suggestions which leave out testing for speed altogether but rather concentrate on the most skillful arrival at the finishing line.

Riding the bicycle for technical skill involves tasks that have been agreed in advance (picking up a handkerchief while riding, turning on the spot, riding with one hand etc.).

BMX style bikes have been built to take the extra wear and tear involved in 'trick' cycling. The sturdy frame and wheels are ideal for the skills which can be performed when you know your bike and how to perform with it. It is, of course, always advisable to wear protective clothing for this style of bike riding.

Rolling in the summer and gliding in

Both roller and ice skates have much in common. For beginners on the skates falling down is a constant hazard. That doesn't matter — if you know how to fall. Therefore a tip in advance: learn it as quickly as possible.

But there are a few more rules to observe before you can begin. You must be very careful when skating in road traffic as even the most skillful skater can fall in front of a car. The driver won't be able to stop quickly enough for you to escape injury. Therefore, think first, then look, then skate. But on the ice, of course, you are safe from cars. But here, too, there is a rule which you shouldn't disregard. Even the smoothest ice surface can be fragile, once it has broken under your weight it can quickly lead to a catastrophe. So, only skate on ice that has been passed as safe for ice skaters.

Most of the games here are as suitable for roller skating as for ice skating. If you have gained a little experience why not play 'catch the hat'. Each skater wears a hat of some sort which must be caught by the others. Whoever catches the most hats is the winner. Or you can play with two teams against each other. Which team is going to win the game?

Basket ball

Roller or ice skating leaves your hands free. They can be used for playing. Place a basket, bucket or similar thing in a convenient spot. Now draw a spiral with five rings around the basket (like in the illustration). Each skater starts at the outer ring. Skating around each circle a ball is thrown which he must catch and throw into the basket. Catching it means 5 points in the outer circle, 4 points in the fourth circle and so on. Hitting the basket receives 10, 8, 6, 4, 2 points — and if the ball stays in the basket that means 25, 20, 15, 10 and 5 points according to the circle.

Hockey — a game for summer and winter

Hockey is a fast game, and usually quite rough. You need a playing pitch, a ball, or a puck on ice — and two teams with at least three players each. A referee could be useful, too — he's usually the most important person on the hockey field.

Each team selects a goalkeeper. He is the only one allowed to touch the ball or puck with his hands. All the others play the field. They carry sticks with which they try to drive the ball across the field and into the goal.

The player driving the ball can be prevented by the opponents using the whole body. But beating with the stick and tripping up count as a 'foul' which is penalised by a free hit for the other team. Touching the ball with the hand is also a foul.

You can either play for time, say twice 10 minutes. Or you can determine that the winning team will be the first to score ten goals. And you must observe the rules of the game. No opponent is allowed between the goalkeeper and his defender (otherwise a player might just stand there the whole time waiting for an 'easy goal'). If

the winter . . .

Slalom, sprint and others . . .

For a slalom, skating sticks are stuck into the ice or stones placed on the ground. These must be circled from left to right towards the next stick. The winner is the one who skates up and down the course fastest and without a mistake. An interesting variation is the 'parallel-slalom'. For this you set up two identical slalom courses. Two skaters start at the same time rivalling each other. The winner goes through to the next race.

For the sprint you need an oval space with two tracks. The tracks must be open at the broad sides. At these openings the skaters change tracks so that its not always the same person to skate on the outside track. Do a competition with several rounds. Each time eliminating the loser.

possible try to build up some sort of boundaries behind the goals so that the ball can bounce back.

The art of skating

True masters of skates can do the most impressive tricks. You can watch the art of these skaters during championships – and you probably won't understand any of the terms used in this event. Who knows what a Double Rittberger or a Salcho or whatever else is? You don't need that, really. The art of skating begins by being able to stand or glide on one foot. And to complete a figure of eight on the ice or ground is not as easy as it looks.

Try to skate curves by shifting your own weight – on one leg. Once you can do that place a stick on the ground, take a run and jump over it. Now try to twist round when you are over the stick in the air. Try to do the same while landing with the same foot you jumped off with. Does it work? Then you can skate quite well! Next is a pirouette – turning on the spot. You need quite a lot of momentum here, too. If you manage to twist around twice while in the air over the stick, land on the same leg and immediately do a pirouette then you are on the road to becoming a champion!

Skateboard know-how

The skateboard is, like its 'younger brother' the skate, an invention from America. The points listed here are applicable to both:

Driving a skateboard is an attractive but also dangerous pastime. That's why we have to say a few words here. It is worthwhile reading the next few lines and carefully studying the drawings on the right.

Ideally buy your skateboard accompanied by an adult. Carefully check that the board surface isn't too slippery, that the edges and screws aren't sharp or pointed. And then practice, to begin with, in places where there is no traffic. Getting on and off, pushing off, turning and winding are all described on the next page. Once you know these techniques . . .

. . . you are still not ready for riding off. Now you need a set of protective clothing. Look at the boy in the picture — and the clothing and equipment he's wearing:

1. The head is protected by a helmet. The head can be badly injured during a fall.
2. He wears elbow protectors, as the joints must be specially protected against falling.
3. That's why he also wears knee protectors. The knees are usually grazed on the road surface when falling off the skateboard.
4. He wears high fitting sneakers (basket ball shoes) to protect the ankles.

Skateboard games

You can play many games with your friends on skateboards but you can play on your own just as well. Set up a slalom course and try to master it in the shortest time without mistakes. Or try to skate down some steps. With others, you can organise a rally or a parallel-slalom. A skateboard obstacle course could also be made. But, in danger, immediately interrupt your game and dismount!

The great pentathlon

The pentathlon is a five-part race and should be done on a field for five participants. You need a race track about 50 metres long. With chalk, draw five parallel tracks on the ground. Now all that's needed is a referee and you can begin.

1. run: Peter starts on roller skates, Susan on the bicycle, Andrew on the skateboard, Lucy on foot and James on one roller skate. The five times are taken with a stop watch and noted down.

2. run: Now each competitor moves up one track — Susan starts on roller skates, Andrew on the bicycle, Lucy on the skateboard, James on foot and Peter on one roller skate. Again, all times are taken and noted.

After five runs, that is after each competitor has run in each 'discipline' the seconds are added up. The competitor with the lowest overall time is the winner.

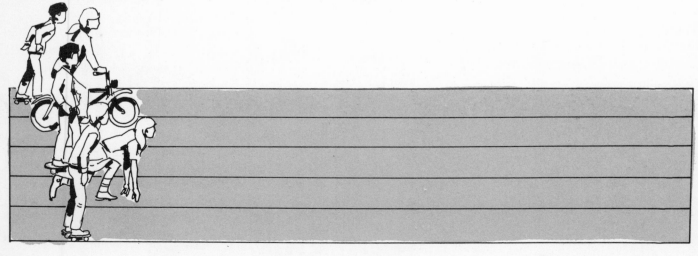

Brief skateboard lesson

Getting on
Step on the board with one leg, push away with the other leg and place both legs on the board. Position your feet across the board to have a better grip. One foot must be placed just behind the first pair of wheels, the other almost on the rear pair of wheels.

Getting off
Practice getting off on a level surface at first. Once you can do that try it on a hill. You have to plan ahead before stopping. Take your right leg off the board and swing it before the skateboard while shifting your weight backwards. Then place your right foot on the ground and move your weight onto that foot.

Pushing off
The easiest way of moving about on a skateboard is pushing yourself. It's similar to a scooter without the handlebar to hold on to. Take your right leg off the board and push it down on the ground beside the board. Leave your foot there until your whole body is pushed forward.

Turning
Turnings and curves are driven by shifting your body weight. Step onto the board and shift your weight to the side so that your centre of gravity is to the left of the board. Keep your balance by spreading your arms. By shifting your weight to the back the board will lift at the front enabling you to steer it.

Winding
On the rolling board place your feet as far apart as possible. Shift your weight to the back and with your front leg move the front wheels by 180°. Set down gently and try the same with the rear end. You have to shift your weight from side to side continuously.

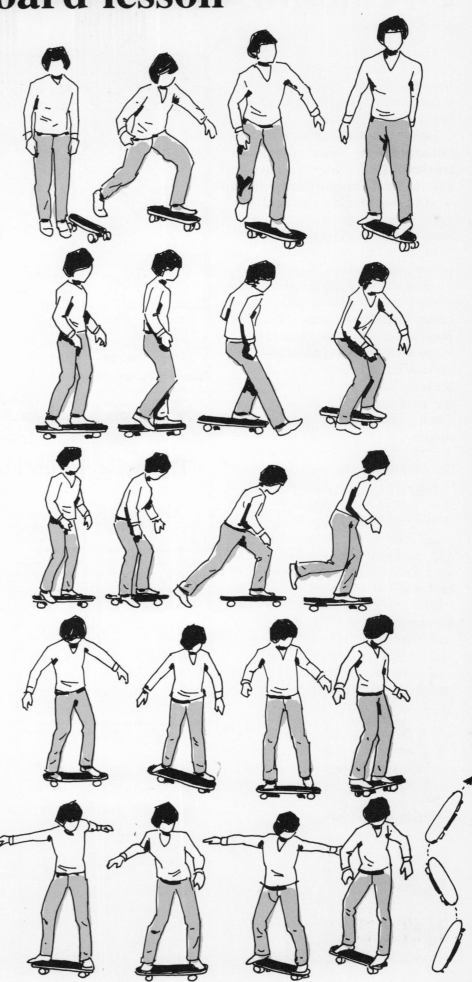

Great fun with a calculator

The calculator is a good toy. Nowadays one of these mini-computers can be found in almost every household.

Before we start, here is a short introduction if you have never used one before:-

Most calculators, although often of quite different appearance, have eight digits, that means they can show figures up to 99,999,999. That is quite sufficient for our games.

The calculator has different keys which are pressed once it is switched on. Number keys are from 0 to 9, and there is a key for a point which symbolises the decimal point. Then there are the keys for the four main rules of arithmetic: addition +, subtraction −, multiplication x and division ÷.

There is a key for = which starts the arithmetic process, and the C which cancels out the numbers if you've gone wrong or you want to start something else.

The figure on the key you press will appear on the display area at the top of the calculator. When you press one of the arithmetic keys the figure remains. It only changes when a problem is in progress or finished.

Try it for yourself

Now enough of words, try it for yourself. You want to do 2 + 3. Press the key for 2 and it appears in the window. Press + and the 2 remains. Now press 3. When you then press = the 5 will appear in the display. That's it.

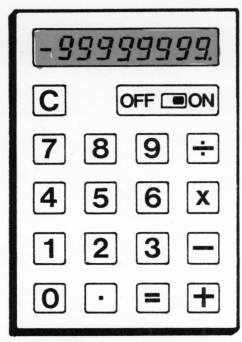

Second move, subtraction. Press 9, then −, then 6, then =. What have you got? 3! Therefore: 9−6=3.

Now try multiplication. How much is 4x5? 20, you'll see. Press 4, then x, and then 5. After pressing = the 20 will appear in the window.

Division you can do without the illustration, can't you? Well, how much is 24÷8? Press 2, then 4, now the display is 24. Next press ÷ and then 8. Press = and what is the result? Correct, 3!

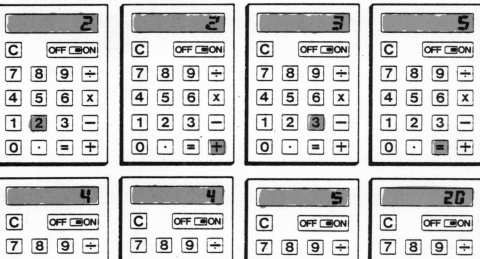

A calculator that can write

You can make your calculator write some words. With a little imagination, once you have learnt the numbers which can convert to letters, you can write several words. Try these to start with: Remember, you have to turn the calculator upside down to read the words.

Press the keys in this order exactly:

0.7734 = hello
3705 = sole
77345 = shell
3045 = shoe
710 = oil
35006 = goose
5507 = loss
35007 = loose
Now try some of your own!

The wicked 21

For this game you need a partner, a calculator, notepaper and a pen. Each one of you presses a number between 1 and 9 in turn. Between each number the + symbol is pressed every time. The aim of the game is to display the number 21 in the window. The winner is the one who presses the last number after which the figure 21 appears. Each number may only be pressed once!

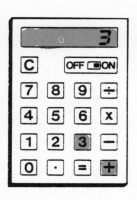 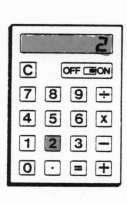 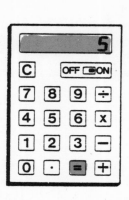 

Above, Peter has pressed 3 and written it down on the notepaper. Now Susan adds 2 and the figure 5 appears.

  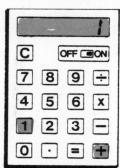 

The 2 is noted. Peter adds 5, writes it down, and the 10 appears. Susan presses 1, writes it down, and 11 is displayed.

 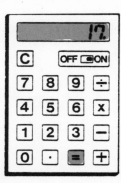 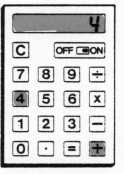 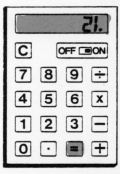

Peter tries the number 6, the window says 17. Now Susan can press the 4: and 21 is reached. Susan wins!

Play strategy

As Peter added the 6 he lost the game. In the second round the result was 11 with the 3, 2, 5 and 1 gone, and 4, 6, 7, 8 and 9 remaining. From 11 to 21 was 10. So Peter shouldn't have used either 4 or 6 as Susan could reply with a 6 or 4 to make 21. The only way for Peter to win the game was to add the larger figures: 7, 8 or 9. Then Susan wouldn't have been able to reach 21 and a new game would have had to be played. Therefore, this game must be played with a certain strategy, two or three steps must be planned in advance. And remember, each number may only be used once.

Let's overload

The game 'overload' can be played with two or more players. Each should have a calculator. In addition you will need two dice. Here we explain the basic rules and on the right we go through a match. The aim of the game is, as the name implies, to try and overload the calculator.

The dice are rolled and the player rolling the highest number begins by pressing it into his calculator (12 is the highest). If a player rolls two equal numbers everyone rolls the dice again and adds the new figure to the first.

Bad luck

If you throw a double (after the start), that is a pair of two equal numbers, that is bad luck. You must divide the figure on the display of your calculator by the number on your dice.

Success

If you roll an uneven number you've had success. You can multiply the new number with the one on the calculator.

Luck

If the sum of your dice is 7 or 11 you multiply that with the figure in your calculator and throw the dice again.

And now a sample match:-

Alice	Peter	Susan

1. Round

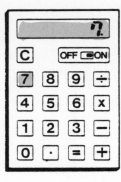 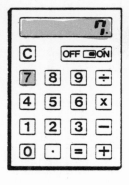 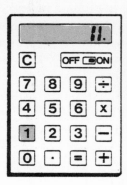

Alice rolls 3/4. She presses 7.	Peter rolls 6/1. He also presses 7.	Susan rolls 5/6. She presses 11 and starts the next round.

2. Round

Alice rolls 4/5. She presses $7 \times 9 = 63$.	Peter rolls 4/4. He has BAD LUCK and presses $7 \div 8 = 0.875$.	Susan rolls 1/6. She has LUCK, presses $11 \times 7 = 77$ and rolls the dice again: 1/2. That's 77×3. The display now shows 231.

3. Round

Alice rolls 2/5. That is LUCK. She presses $63 \times 7 = 441$ and rolls the dice again. Now she has 4/5, that is $441 \times 9 = 3,969$.	Now Peter is on a lucky streak. He first rolls 2/5, then 3/4, then 1/6 and then 1/5. That is $0.875 \times 7 = 6.125 \times 7 = 42.875 \times 7 = 300.125 \times 6 = 1,800.75$. He's caught up.	Susan rolls 2/6 and presses $231 \times 8 = 1,848$.

4. Round

Alice's fourth round is a 4/5. She presses $3,969 \times 9 = 35,721$.	Peter is fighting splendidly: 3/4. So it's $1,800.75 \times 7 = 12,605.25$. Then 3/5, that's $\times 8 = 100,842$.	Now Susan presses in her new number: 2/5. So $1,848 \times 7 = 12,936$. Then 1/6. The same again: $12,936 \times 7 = 90,552$. Then she has BAD LUCK. She rolls 5/5 and has to divide by 10, that makes 9,055.2.

Thus the game continues until one of the three players 'overloads' his calculator and shows that he has a letter in his display window (the letter varies with the type of calculator, it could be C, E, K or whatever). The winner is awarded a point. Five more games are played and at the end all the points are added up. The one with the most points is the overall winner!

The amazing multiplication trick

There was a clever man who thought up something interesting. It was a calculator trick with which you can puzzle your friends – a new type of multiplication!

The exercise is 84x77. Now you continue as shown in the top left hand box. You divide always by 2. Thus, by dividing, always rounding down, you'll get the numbers 84, 42, 21, 10, 5, 2 and 1. Write these down on a piece of paper. Now take the other figure, 77. With that you do exactly the opposite, you multiply by 2. That makes 77, 154, 308, 616, 1,232, 2,464 and 4,928. Now write both columns of figures next to each other and cross out all the figures divisible by two from the first column and the corresponding figures of the second column. Add up the remaining figures and compare the result!

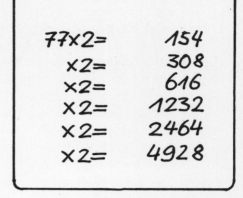

$$84 \div 2 = (42) \quad 42$$
$$\div 2 = (21) \quad 21$$
$$\div 2 = (10.5) \quad 10$$
$$\div 2 = (5.25) \quad 5$$
$$\div 2 = (2.625) \quad 2$$
$$\div 2 = (1.3125) \quad 1$$

$$77 \times 2 = \quad 154$$
$$\times 2 = \quad 308$$
$$\times 2 = \quad 616$$
$$\times 2 = \quad 1232$$
$$\times 2 = \quad 2464$$
$$\times 2 = \quad 4928$$

$$\begin{array}{ll} \cancel{84} & \cancel{77} \\ \cancel{42} & \cancel{154} \\ 21 & 308 \\ \cancel{10} & \cancel{616} \\ 5 & 1232 \\ \cancel{2} & \cancel{2464} \\ 1 & 4928 \end{array}$$

$$\begin{array}{r} 308 \\ +1232 \\ +4928 \\ \hline =6468 \end{array}$$

And again in case you don't believe it . . .

Incredible, isn't it. The multiplication of 84 and 77 makes 6,468. And adding up the numbers 308, 1,232 and 4,928 what is the result? That's right, the same: 6,468. Magic?

Let's try it with another figure to see whether it was just an accident or whether this funny way of arithmetic is always correct. 66x95? OK. So: 66, 33, 16, 8, 4, 2 and 1 are on the left hand side, and 95, 190, 380, 760, 1,520, 3,040 and 6,080 on the other. What is the result when added up? 6,270. And multiplied? 6,270. They look the same!

And you needn't always have two digit numbers, you can take any number you wish. Now, go and puzzle your maths teacher or your parents.

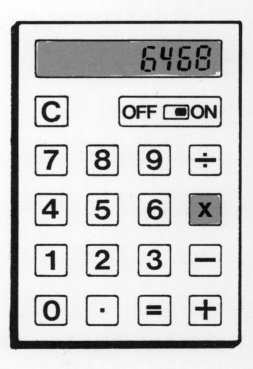

Music as a hobby?

But that isn't all! You can write music yourself, it's called *composing*. When whistling your own tune you are already composing – if you haven't pinched the tune from somewhere else, that is. To think up a tune isn't that difficult. The hard bit is to keep it. Part of this chapter deals with that (you need notes and rhythm . . .).

Finally we describe here how you can work with other people's music by recording it on tape or cassette and then 'cutting' and 'mixing' it.

Jazz

Jazz has developed from American negro music. Black people brought from Africa as slaves, and their descendants, blended African and American music and played it on their own instruments. There are many forms of jazz, from the jolly dance music of Dixieland to the melancholy blues, which echo the old slave songs. The particular characteristics of jazz are its strong rhythm and *improvisation*, which is when the performers add their own ideas during the performance.

Why does a whole long chapter of this hobby book deal with music? Well, music can be a hobby, too. It's an important subject. You can do a lot with music: to begin with you can *listen* to music; there are, indeed, a lot of possibilities. There's music from the radio, television, from records, tapes and cassettes. But these are just 'canned', (recorded music). Music is also available 'live', from pop concerts, orchestral performances, the opera hall, church choirs and brass bands in the park.

But listening is one thing, to *make* music yourself is another. You can sing, play an instrument, play in a band with others, and you can drum about on various tin cans. Making music can be much more fun than listening to music made by others.

Hopefully you'll have an idea by now about the many possibilities of making music your hobby. Many people are occupied with music, from soldiers in a military band to the street busker.

Classical

Composers over the centuries have written a great deal of orchestral music; they transformed moods and feelings into melodies as well as theatrical dramas (operas). We describe this music as classical or serious music. Perhaps you have heard of composers such as Bach, Mozart and Beethoven? Classical music is part of European culture. There are works for orchestras; trios and quartets for three or four instruments; music for choirs, and solo pieces for particular instruments, such as the piano.

Orchestras and their

An orchestra consists of several groups of instruments. There are the 'strings' (violin, viola, cello and double bass), the 'wind instruments' (flute, bassoon,

Folk

Folk is the term for the music of the people. The peoples of each country have their own music which has developed from their culture. In folk music we can find old languages, opinions and traditions, 'pagan' customs and war songs, ballads (stories set to a tune) and love songs. Some folk songs are sung unaccompanied while others are accompanied by instruments like the guitar.

Pop

Pop is the abbreviation of popular music. It includes everything that is currently popular. Anything from 'groups' like Duran Duran and singers like Madonna from various countries are sold under the term pop. Everything revolves around the 'charts', the Top Forty lists that show which singers or groups are most popular at the moment, according to how many records they have sold.

There are many different types of pop music: rock and roll, soul, heavy metal, reggae, jazz-funk, punk, ska . . . the list is endless. The exciting thing about pop music is that it is constantly changing. So much so that every new generation seems to have a sound entirely of its own, which captures the mood of the time. Part of the attraction of pop is choosing your favourite bands or singers and following their fortunes (not to mention their clothes and ideas).

music

clarinet, trumpet, trombone, oboe, horn and tuba) and the 'percussion instruments' (drums, timbal or kettledrum, cymbals and triangle). The orchestra is usually made

complete by the piano or grand piano.

Orchestras are not limited to playing classical music. They sometimes play jazz, military music and many others. Some pop groups have been known to perform with entire orchestras!

Exotic music

We all know what a guitar, drums or a piano looks like. But other countries have different customs. Especially different instruments. These musical instruments are called 'exotic' because they look and sound strange to our ears. But some of these exotic instruments have become quite popular with us. For instance, many people now know what a 'sitar' from India is like.

There are musical instruments one wouldn't believe could make a tune. For example, there is a type of drum in Africa which is tied with ropes. When the ropes are pressed the drum becomes thinner in the middle, so the sound of the drum can be made higher or lower. Entire melodies can be played on these drums. And there are Chinese violins with only one string. When played by an expert they can produce an amazing variety of sounds.

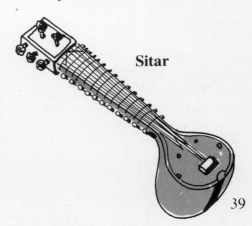

Sitar

What is music?

This is not an easy question to answer. But we don't want to wrestle here with great problems, this is a hobby book and not a scientific textbook. If you are not satisfied with the explanations here (and that would be a good thing) why not go to the local library and find a book about it.

Music is the sequence of different sounds that reach our ears. Music we know sounds familiar, strange music can sound quite terrible to our ears. Every sound that is made by musical instruments or voices is music. Of course, for some people the sound of a motorbike is like music to their ears. But that's not what we are talking about here.

Music consists of various sounds. But what are sounds?

What are sounds?

When you throw a stone into a lake concentric waves will form, as you know. Now imagine that you can make the same effect in the air, too. When you shout out, for example, the vibration of your voice causes the air in front of your mouth to vibrate, too. This 'wave' continues until it reaches the ear of somebody else.

Within the ear is the eardrum. And it does, indeed, act like a drum by conducting the vibrations of the air. These vibrations are perceived as sounds inside the brain. If you make a high noise more vibrations are passed into the air, a low noise makes less. When you make a high, middle and low noise you have created three different sounds.

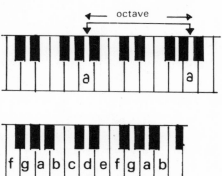

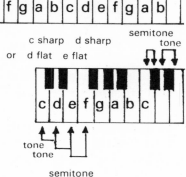

Above you see a diagram of the keyboard of a piano. There are white keys and black keys. Eight white keys make up an 'octave', but between them there are five more black keys. An octave is the range of a register. Take a c and then play the next higher c. You will notice that the sound is similar but a bit higher, a register higher.

The eight white keys are named c, d, e, f, g, a, b, c. But if you can't use either c or d you can take the tone in between (the black key).

Apart from these main tones there are semitones. That is the sound that is a little higher than the c, the c sharp.

What are notes?

But how can tones be transformed so that a musician plays exactly what the composer wants? That is what the language of music, the notation, was invented for; each tone becomes a certain symbol.

The notes are written on lines, with five lines running parallel to each other. These lines are called a

staff. At the beginning of each staff is the clef which tells about the pitch of the tones. The most common clefs are the treble clef and the bass clef. Next to that there are usually some figures which indicate the time or meter of the

music. Each vertical line means that a second has passed. If it says 2 and 4, for example, that means the second is divided in four parts and the stress is on the second and fourth part: ta tam ta tam. The 'belly' of the treble clef encircles the point on which the note g is placed (=5 notes above c).

Now you can read the notes of the first diagram: c, c, d, d, g, g, e, a, a, d, d.

On the diagram below you see the notes spread over two staff systems, the bottom with a bass clef and the top with a treble clef. It's now clear, too, how the notes are described with letters: the low ones with capital letters, then the small letters and the higher notes are written with a small 1, the even higher ones with a small 2 . . .

Melody and rhythm

Well, by now you should be able to write in music a simple melody, 'Frère Jacques' for example: c, d, e, c . . .

But how fast are you going to sing or play this? For that you need something else: notes can be written in different ways because there are so many different speeds a melody can be played.

You know that one unit of time, a bar, lasts one second. A second is quite a long time in musical terms. One must be able to divide it. Composers don't want to make things too difficult, so the notes are always divisible by two:
1 whole note (semibreve) has
2 half notes (minims) or
4 quarter notes (crotchets) or
8 eighth notes (quavers) or
16 sixteenth notes (semiquavers) or
32 thirtysecond notes (demisemiquavers).

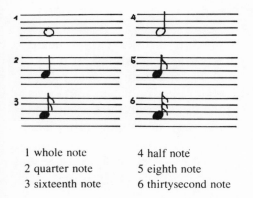

1 whole note	4 half note
2 quarter note	5 eighth note
3 sixteenth note	6 thirtysecond note

And now a little more. If you know a waltz try humming the rhythm: tam ta ta, tam ta ta . . . That's always three notes to a bar. But you can't divide a bar into three . . . That's why there is such a rhythmical feature to the waltz: the 'tam' is a half note or quaver, the 'ta ta' two quarter notes or crotchets. Now you have three notes, but when you add up the time of each (1 half and 2 quarter) you'll get a whole bar. That's how the rhythm can be changed (but there are other ways, too, of course).

Playing an instrument is fun

Playing an instrument is fun, but learning it isn't such fun because you have to practice a lot to get nice sounds from your instrument.

So here is a brief introduction to playing the guitar, on this and the next page. And, of course, you will have to practice fingering and plucking, too.

Let us suppose that you are right-handed. If you are left-handed you will have to reverse the instructions, though there are special guitars for left-hands.

Place the guitar on your lap with your right hand on the strings, near the hole, and your left hand on the neck of the guitar, near the top.

At the top, the pegbox, the strings are fastened to rollers that can be moved by pegs. To begin with you must tune the guitar as the strings continually distort. At first you may be better off using a special tuning whistle. Blowing into that you hear the notes E, A, D, G, B, E.

Tune the strings to these notes.

The neck of the guitar is divided by little metal bars, the frets. The space between two frets is called the course (see diagram). Well, now we can begin, turn to the next page . . .

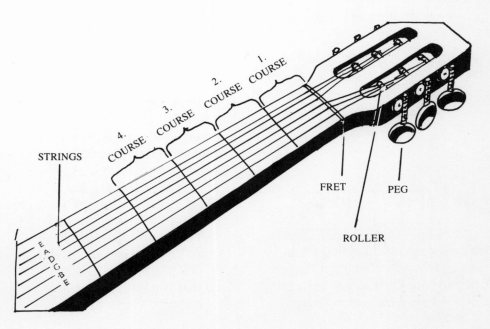

A little practice is necessary . . .

Let's start with the left hand. It is responsible for the notes and the chords. A chord consists of a combination of notes from any of the six strings. Below you'll find a table of various finger positions. That's how you have to place the fingers of your left hand. E major is like this: the index finger on the G-string, 1st course / the middle finger on the D-string, 2nd course / the ring finger on the A-string, 2nd course.

That is the E major chord. Now with the thumb of your right hand pluck at the strings one after the other. Only when all strings sound without clanking can you play 'clean'. Now pluck all the strings once again. Look at the A major chord and try to play it equally well.

Once you can play that try to change. First play E major and count slowly to four, then play A major and count again to four. Try to keep the time between playing the first and second chord in time to your counting so that the time between each chord is no longer than the time between a repeat of the same chord. Once you've mastered changing the chords you can accompany simple songs on your guitar. The right hand is the plucking hand. Plucking means pulling at the strings with your fingers. You can pluck with all your fingers, but it's better with your index finger placed against your thumb. Or you can use a little piece of plastic called a plectrum.

E major

1. course

2. course

3. course

C major

1. course

2. course

3. course

A major

1. course

2. course

3. course

a minor

1. course

2. course

3. course

The making of musical instruments

Now don't be put off when we talk about instrument making. We don't want to go on at length about the finer points of violin making — or keep you from your hobbies. No, this is about ideas for making your own musical instruments.

An instrument needn't always be a great work of art — and often isn't. But being able to make music on an instrument you've made yourself is a great achievement.

You've probably outgrown the stage of beating saucepans. Perhaps you've also tried 'twanging' a ruler from a desk or drawer. You get different sounds depending on how far the ruler is protruding from the desk.

Next is the rubber band guitar. Stretch elastic bands of various sizes over a wooden box, such as a cigar box. On one end place a wooden building block, or similar, to make a 'fret'. Now you can make sounds with the strings of your 'guitar'.

Another simple thing to make is a tin balalaika. Find a small wooden board and nail three nails at the top. Fasten the board at the bottom to a square or rectangular tin — this serves as the 'sound box' increasing the sound waves. Tie a strong wire around the tin to which you can now fasten the strings. The top of the strings tie to the three nails at the top. Now you've built a stringed instrument with which you can actually make music. You can vary the pitch of the different strings by moving your fingers up and down the 'neck' of your balalaika.

With a little experimentation, you can also build a simple flute.

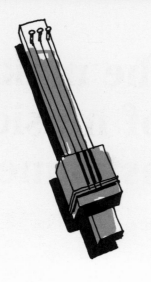

Cut off a length of willow wood and drill holes in it, several on the upper side, one on the underside. Now you have to make a

mouthpiece by drilling a little way into a joint to leave a membrane. By making and trying out several of these flutes you should be able to work out the exact position of the holes so you can actually play some music. Once you have found the right place for the holes you could make a flute from clay by forming the clay exactly like the willow flute. You might find a place to fire the flute, perhaps at school or an adult education centre.

Another musical 'instrument' can be made by filling several

glasses with water. When you rub the rims with a wet finger you can play the 'water organ'.

Simple repairs to the guitar

How about some simple repairs to a damaged guitar?

Case 1: The strings cannot be moved at the rollers. That's quickly fixed. Go to a musical instrument dealer and buy some new rollers. They come in different widths, so it's a good idea to take one of the old ones with you, or to measure the space between the channels before you go, to make sure that you buy the correct size. With a small screwdriver undo the little screws that fastened the rollers to the pegbox (don't forget to take off the strings beforehand). Take out the old roller and insert the new one. Now you can fit your new rollers. Tighten the screws and do the same with the other pegs. Now fix the strings – preferably a new set – and you're ready to play.

Case 2: There's a lot of clanking, and some 'frets' are lost. Take off the strings and remove the old 'frets' You can buy new ones in a musical instrument shop. Now you need some sandpaper (not too coarse), varnish or dark clear lacquer, a wood cutting knife and a piece of iron.

And now? Sand down the neck, fix the new frets in place after re-cutting the grooves, and varnish. Fit the strings and test whether the sound of the guitar is 'true': Pluck the C string over the entire width of the course. If the octaves aren't correct anymore, it's possible that you might have to reposition the bridge on the main body of the guitar.

Case 3: The cover is cracked.

To do the repair yourself, again, you have to begin by taking off the strings and bridge. Brush the gluepoints inside with thinners on a long brush, especially the gluepoints of the support struts. When the glue has dissolved carefully lift off the cover of the sound body.

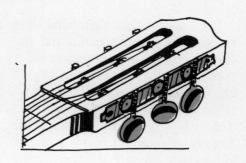

Now you must copy all the pieces. Make a paper pattern of the cover and carefully measure the support struts – preferably make a drawing. Cut new struts from plywood; it's also possible to cut the cover from 3mm plywood but it's really better to buy a new cover from a guitar shop, made of pine perhaps – the sound of your guitar would be much superior.

After carefully removing all the old glue re-apply fresh glue. Fit the support struts and finally fit the new cover in place, fixing it with screwclamps until the glue is dry. Finish off by varnishing the wood and fixing a new bridge on the surface.

To glue a crack in the cover is not advisable – most of the sound will be lost.

Making a bamboo flute

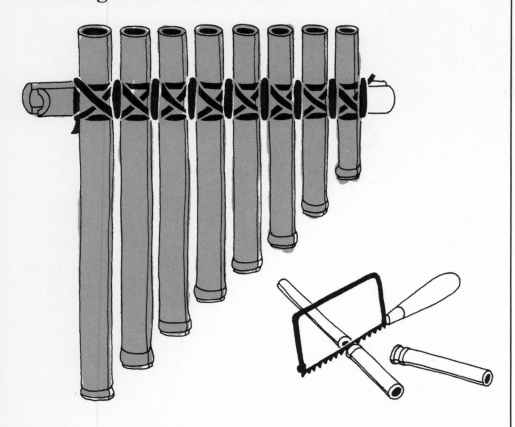

You probably know this instrument from pictures of ancient Greece. It's also called a Pan flute.

Buy yourself some bamboo sticks from a florist. Ask an adult to help you cut off eight pieces with a hacksaw. Make the first cut just above a knot where the wood is thicker. You'll notice there that the pipe is sealed with a 'wall'.

Measure out 23cm from the first cut and cut off the piece. Now you have the first flutepipe with an open end. Cut seven further pieces each 1cm shorter than the one before. The eighth piece should be just about 15cm long. Now you need a piece of bamboo that is longer than the eight pipes laid side by side. This piece shouldn't have a knot. Cut this pipe in half lengthwise and smooth the edges with sand paper.

The eight flutes are tied with a strong piece of string between the two halves, as illustrated in the diagram.

If the grading of the tones isn't correct you have to shorten the flutes until the scale is right.

To play it, press the bamboo flute vertically against your lips and blow the air over the openings and not into them.

Music tricks and technology

In the nineteen-sixties stereo or hi-fi technology really took off, and has continued to become more and more sophisticated. (Hi-fi means high fidelity or the true reproduction of sound.) Only a few years ago one would think oneself lucky to be the owner of an old two-track tape recorder.

Nowadays it has to be a four-track reel recorder with multiplayback. Whereas before, the music reached our ear through a large 'wireless' with tubes over the ether waves, today we have combinations of elements like 'tuners' and 'amplifiers', cassette decks and record players all in one unit. And with the addition of two or even four speakers the equipment can take up over a third of the room.

Naturally, to record music that isn't transferred from a record or radio you need proper equipment. But that doesn't mean you have to spend hundreds of pounds. It is also possible to record, play over and devise radio plays with the aid of just a radio and a tape recorder.

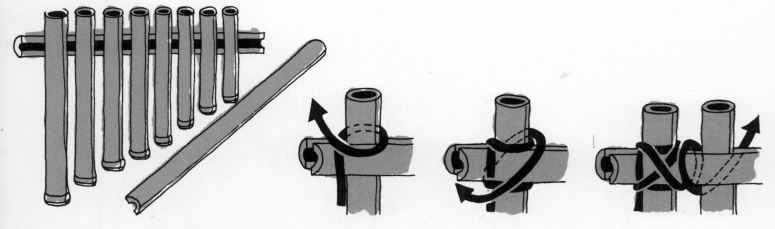

Recording, copying, composing, radio plays etc.

Recording methods vary from equipment to equipment so there is no point in explaining just one of many here. Either follow the instructions for your set or, if they are lost, just work it out by trial and error by yourself. That's more fun anyway as you can really 'explore' the machine.

For all interesting experiments you basically need two recorders. The same with the most simple activity, copying. Get together with a friend who also has a recorder and you can start. One recorder plays back the tape while the other records it (you must, of course, connect the two recorders beforehand). You will need a second recorder if you want to create what's called 'multi-tracking'. One recorder plays back the tape while the other records it, plus your own additions, with a microphone.

To create different sound effects for radio plays look at the following page. Here we want to return to the recording of music you have played yourself.

If you want to record your own singing voice and an instrument together you will have no difficulties using a stereo recorder. One mike records one track, the second the other track. But if you want to record from more than two sources you will need a mixer. You select which source should go on to what channel and you combine them by directing several microphones into the mixer and guide them into the two channels according to your wishes. Do a few trial runs at first, changing the sound quality and channel combinations until everything is correct. And then: attention, recording in progress!

You won't, of course, have enough money to buy your own stereo equipment. But you might have some in your living room. If your parents are worried about you touching the equipment, why don't you ask them to show you properly so that you know exactly how to work it.

The amplifier

This is the centre of your equipment and responds to 'watts'. The more watts the prouder the owner. But seriously, a good amplifier should have twice 35 watts and several connector points for radio, speakers, record deck, tape and cassette recorders.

The receiver

As good as it may be, the amplifier can only amplify what it receives. If you want to make good radio recordings you must have a decent receiver, preferably one that can eliminate background noise. Whether it has pre-programming, digital display or other finer features depends mainly on taste and finance.

The record player

Most decisions for or against a particular system are matters of opinion. Whether a direct-drive or belt-drive turntable is better — who wants to decide that? Most important is a decent head, preferably with a diamond stylus. And the record must be clean!

The tape recorder

It is more complicated than the cassette deck mentioned below. But it provides many more possibilites, whether for multi-tracking (where you could fill up a track with many recordings, even simulate an entire orchestra on your own, like Mike Oldfield) or with a trick button. But a good tape recorder is very expensive.

The cassette deck

It has almost driven out the tape recorder for the ordinary consumer — because the cassette deck is easy to operate. Pay special attention to the 'tape select' switch which you adjust to the type of your cassette (chrome or ferro cassette). And a 'dolby' system would be useful, too, to eliminate background noise.

The mixer

If you want to mix different sound sources like two microphones, record and cassette, you really need a mixer. You can determine the different sound elements just as you want the finished tape. Mixers can be bought as kits which can be assembled at home.

Speakers and accessories

Speakers should withstand more watts than are emitted by the amplifier. You must decide which speakers to buy by listening to the various types. Important accessories are connector cables, microphones and headsets, and of course cassettes and tapes — if you want to become more professional you also want a cutting device for your tapes. And other useful things are supports for the microphones, called gallows. You have probably seen them in television studios.

Now let's start . . .

Music tricks and technology

What use is the best 'script' for your radio play if it doesn't sound real? Horses trampling across the prairies, thunder and banging. Ships' horns must toot, doors squeak and so on. We now want to introduce you to the art of sound making.

Box of tricks

A marching batallion can be simulated with cellophane or foil, as can the departure of a train, just crumple it up. Balloons can create rubbing and whistling sounds. Or you can fill the balloons with little balls (dried peas or lentils, etc.) to create the sound of the sea.

Trotting horses

You need the two halves of a coconut shell. Now set down the halves in varying rhythms onto different surfaces to simulate the varying terrain the horse encounters. You could use sand, felt, pebbles, water . . .

Fire

Again you will need cellophane or foil. Crumpled very slowly it sounds like an open fire. Working faster and breaking matchsticks as well, it soon sounds like a forest fire.

Creepy footsteps

With leather soles step on a creaking floor board. If you play back the recorded sound on half speed and add some echo it will sound like hollow, creeping footsteps.

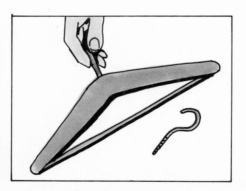

Squeaking door

Perhaps you have a squeaking door at home. Otherwise use a wooden coat hanger. Unscrew the metal hook and screw in a wooden peg. Turning the wood inside the wood makes a horrible sound.

Wind

Blowing gently across the microphone sounds like wind. Using the balloon again that wind becomes a storm. And to create a hurricane swing a stone tied to a piece of string round and round in the air. Make sure it is tied securely!

Lift (Elevator)

To simulate the sound of a lift you can use a vacuum cleaner or electric coffee mill. And imitate the sound of the doors opening and closing by rolling a toy car or castor across a table.

Screams

Writing a script for a play you might need to use screams of horror. Record the crying of a baby and play it back at half speed. Add a little echo . . .

Harbour

You know how to simulate the sounds of wind and water. You can create waves by moving your hand in a bowl or bathtub of water. And the noise of a ship's horn is made by blowing on bottles filled with varying amounts of water.

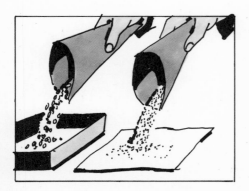

Rain

You want rain? Then pour some rice from a bag into an empty cardboard box. Or sprinkle sugar on a sheet of drawing paper or cellophane. Rice falling onto thin metal foil sounds like hail.

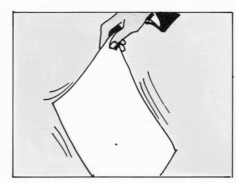

Thunder

If you haven't any thin metal foil, a thick sheet of cardboard is just as good. For thunder hold the cardboard at one corner and shake it a bit. That 'thunders' beautifully, especially with added echo.

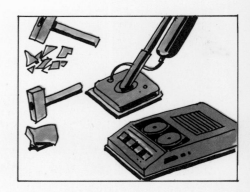

Factory

Take a hammer and knock on glass, stone or wood. Then switch on the coffee mill and vacuum cleaner. Mix it all together on the tape.

Camps and Castles

Who isn't itching to get outside when the weather is nice? Woods, lakes and playgrounds beckon you to play in them as much as you fancy. Whether it's Trapper Vulturebeak fighting it out with Chief Red River, or knights in shining armour proudly riding through the land; whether giants and dwarfs compare their strength, or pirates look for booty and fanciful engineers build incredible dams and bridges, who cares?

But it would be a pity if you had to interrupt or discontinue your play because of bad weather, when the gang has to break up just because it's raining. That's where a self-built shelter comes in — where you can have your meetings and at the same time hide your prisoners, where you can store provisions for bad times and where the Medicine Man prepares himself for the Great Dance of the Seven Rats. This is your place, here you can meet and make final preparations for the great raid on those cheeky palefaces in the neighbourhood.

You want to know what you can build? Well, tents, treecamps, shrub huts, wooden sheds, caves — and in the winter a proper Eskimo igloo entirely made from snow and ice (you'll be surprised how warm and cosy it can be in such icy surroundings)!

But, of course, building such a place is only half the story. It must be completely hidden from the prying eyes of enemies, and therefore well camouflaged. Entry holes and secret escape routes must be constructed and safety features installed right round the camp; leaf traps, ropes and wires.

When choosing a position for your hut make sure it adapts to the conditions of the selected spot. A wooden hut right on top of a sandpile wouldn't deceive the most stupid enemy! But it's more difficult to find a treehouse within a huge old oak tree, especially if it can only be reached by a rope ladder. And a tent must receive a coat of camouflage paint!

So, have a good discussion about the plan and think of all the problems. Remember that trees provide good protection from nosy eyes in the summer because of the foliage, but in the winter they are bare and without protection. Have a contingency camp somewhere else. It isn't unknown to find that you have traitors within the rank and file!

Trackers

Trackers usually prefer solid huts. In the illustrations above you can see the different stages in the erection of such a hut.

Select six thick sticks of about the same length from the woods. Ram these into the ground in the form of a rectangle so that they are sturdy enough to hold you when you lean against them.

Measure out the length of your hut and look for four or six more sticks. These are used to make the roof.

Now you all have to go and find lots of twigs and branches to fill in the walls of your hut, so that there aren't any empty spaces apart from the entrance.

For a door you could nail a few boards together or make one the same way you built the hut. Or you could just use an old blanket in an emergency.

Now you have to camouflage the hut well so it isn't visible to passers-by. That's done with more twigs, leaves or cakes of mud.

Giants + dwarfs

Giants habitually choose their home in the tall caves within rocks. These can be difficult to find. So it's possibly easier to be a dwarf.

The best place to make an artificial cave is between some sturdy boulders. You can construct the sides the same way as the trappers but it will have some of the walls there already. All you have to do is camouflage it.

Red Indians

Red Indians usually live in tents called tepees. For these you'll need a few sticks, about 2m long, and different pieces of fabric.

The erection of a tepee is so simple that it can be taken down and built at another place within minutes — a great advantage.

Join three or four sticks at the top with rope. Then you cover them from top to bottom with fabric, scarves etc. Ideally they should be sewn together. The entrance is formed by a slit in the front. Ready!

At the lake, river or seaside . . .

It is always safest to ask the help of a parent or adult when playing near water. The other thing you must always remember is that smaller children may want to join in your game. Always make sure they can swim and that an adult is watching over them. Water can be dangerous at any age but especially with small children who may get excited and a little too confident.

You can divert a pool of water from the stream to hold fish, or construct a waterfall, or divert the stream into a different direction. You can design a drainage system by a series of different ditches. And you can observe ducks and other waterfowl by carefully stalking through the reeds.

Very good swimmers could build a raft and row it to the centre of the lake where they lower heavy stones tied to ropes into the water. That provides a little island right in the lake. Check the current of the water and direction of the wind beforehand, though.

A moated castle for one day

When you go to a nice sandy beach in the summer, there is a good use for all that sand: it provides the building material for moated castles.

Build a big castle with turrets and walls, walkways and bridges. Dig a moat around the castle. And finally construct a channel which diverts the water from the sea into the moat.

You could organise a competition in castle-building. Everybody works feverishly on the beach, cutting out elaborate turrets and sticking in little flags. Obviously you'll need a committee of judges, made up of children, who decide which castle deserves a prize.

But don't be upset if you cannot find your castle the next day. When the tide comes in it will wash it away. This can sometimes happen while you're still building it.

Outdoors and Indoors

Photography
Angling
Flowers and
flowerbeds
Detective
Kites

Pen friends
Autograph book
Diary
Optical illusion
Pets
Cooking

Picture the world

Photography is a popular hobby, but it can be far more than just that. With photographs you can capture your world in a picture, illustrate a problem to others, produce presents and play at being a reporter.

Photography has come a long way since its beginning nearly 150 years ago. Technological advances have made the most amazing things possible by simply pressing a button. These days, photography as a hobby is not too difficult, as you'll see over the next few pages.

You'll need a camera; but it is not only unnecessary but also silly to buy an expensive camera to begin with; a simple pocket camera for a few pounds is quite good enough.

Once you have got your camera – an old one of your parents' or a friend's is quite sufficient – buy yourself some film. Black and white is the cheapest, but can be expensive to have developed. It should be 18 or 21 DIN (around 135 ASA). Practice taking as many pictures as possible, snap still or moving subjects, in all weathers, everywhere. Then study the prints for mistakes.

How to load the film

If you haven't got a cartridge camera you have to insert the film. Open the camera and insert the cassette with the new film in the left chamber and let the rewind knob click into place. Pull the perforated film towards the right and lay it across the film sprockets. Fold over the beginning of the film and fasten it into the take-up spool on the right; wind on the film two or three times until it is stretched tight over the two spools. Close the camera and advance the film until the '1' appears in the exposure counter window. After winding you have to press the shutter otherwise you can't move the advance lever!

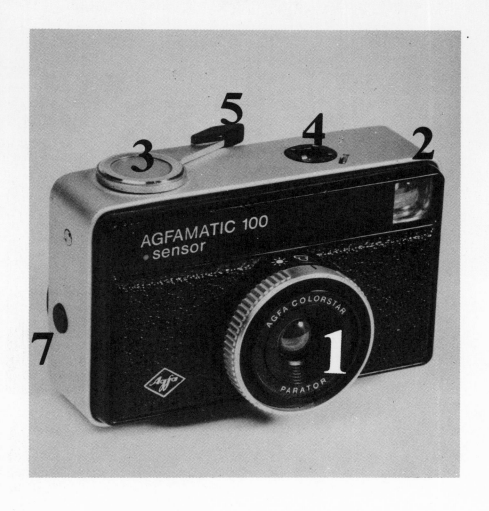

1 The lens

The lens lets in the light from the outside and exposes it to the light-sensitive film within the camera. The glass of the lens must always be clear of grease and dust. So keep it clean.

2 The viewfinder

You must look through the viewfinder to see your subject. Take care to include everything in the viewfinder that you want on your finished print.

3 The shutter release

Before taking a photograph you must wind on the film advance lever. Now the camera is cocked. If you now press the shutter release button light falls into the camera, exposing the film and the picture is 'taken'.

4 The hot shoe

An electronic flash gun or flash cube is slipped into the hot shoe if you want to take pictures in a dark room where additional light is required.

5 The film advance lever

The film advance lever or button is connected with the right-hand spool within the camera. If activated it turns so far that the next picture appears behind the lens.

6 The exposure counter

Looking into the window you can see exactly which picture is on the film at the moment — and then work out how many pictures are still left.

7 Camera back release button

This opens the camera. Only use it when the entire film is on the right spool and the film is finished.

53

We all make mistakes — how can they be avoided?

Too much light isn't the answer, either

The same problem occurs with too much light. When you look straight into the sun or into a strong light you can adjust to it by squinting. And you can do the same with a good camera — by closing the 'aperture' causing the infalling light to go through a smaller hole. But a simple camera won't have that feature. You have to control the infalling light with your hand or not hold the camera directly into the light source.

Keep your fingers off the lens

When taking photographs you look through the viewfinder and therefore cannot see whether the lens is obstructed or dirty. Covering the lens with your finger or your hair is easily done. You must concentrate when taking photographs so you end up with the picture you intended. And take great care that the lens isn't greasy — even rubbing it with a finger makes it greasy so use a cloth instead.

Dark light – dark print

Whenever you want to take a picture of something remember that the camera isn't as sensitive as the human eye. What you can see with your eyes in a fairly dark room the camera might not be able to pick up because its light sensitivity (or rather that of the film within) isn't as great as the eye's. You either have to use a flash or another light source like lights or reflectors.

Keeping calm makes good pictures

When taking a picture you must have a steady hand otherwise the picture will turn out blurred, like the photograph on the left. But the steadiest hand is no good if you don't stand still yourself. So don't stand on a swinging bridge or take photographs out of a moving vehicle. Experienced photographers often set the camera on a firm surface or use a tri-pod onto which they screw the camera.

Your subject might be too fast

A simple camera reacts to a speed of up to a 50th of a second. That sounds quite fast but isn't really. If you want to snap somebody on a bike take the picture from the front. When taken from the side the picture will turn out blurred. Or try to follow the movement of your subject with the camera as you snap.

Don't cut off heads and feet

The most common mistake of budding photographers is to cut off some part of the anatomy . . . On snaps of a party it can be seen over and over again: friends are photographed without heads (at least in the picture). The feet of entire families are cut off. Why? Step back a little bit and you'll have complete people on your picture. You must take care to include everything in the viewfinder.

All about trick photography, panoramic views and photo services . . .

The trick with the perspective

You can trick the people looking at your photos by using the perspective. In the picture on the right you see a child standing on the palm of a hand. Is she a dwarf? No, but the person taking the picture used the perspective by holding her own hand in front of the camera far away from the child. You can see that on the picture below. The same can be done by 'holding' towers or houses . . .

The panoramic view

The camera cannot take as wide a view from, say, the countryside as the human eye, without complicated additional lenses. Therefore we must use a trick. We set the camera on a sturdy surface like a tripod or a pile of bricks — but it must be completely level. Then we take a picture, turn the camera to the centre, snap again and repeat the same again from the right angle. We cut the prints and put them together for a panoramic view.

The mirror trick

You can produce the mirror trick by using the corner of a shop window. The child in the picture doesn't really jump into the air. One arm and one leg are the mirror image of the other limbs. Try to use the mirror trick for other funny photos, too, like faces or objects.

The photo-story

You can tell a story with a sequence of photographs, write a 'photo-novel' or report on problems at your school. You can use different sized pictures, underlay them with coloured paper and insert speech bubbles or write some text underneath. You could

also produce a photo-story as a present for your parents, perhaps of a family holiday. And you can collect photographs for a photo album.

Fish, fresh fish

Two-and-a-half thousand million years ago water vapour mixed with other gases erupted from the crust of the Earth. That caused a layer of clouds many miles thick which covered the sky. And for centuries there was continuous rainfall. At first the falling water evaporated because the Earth was too hot. Then the temperature of the Earth decreased and less water evaporated. As the biggest rainfall the Earth has ever known stopped, two-thirds of the Earth's Surface was covered with water.

All life began in the water. And about 700 million years ago the first ancestors of vertebrate (backboned) animals evolved. Bony fish developed for the first time about 300 million years ago.

Man has always found food in the water. Nothing tastes better than a fish you've caught yourself, grilled over an open fire or fried in a frying pan at home. So why not start fishing?

Where would be the easiest place for you to fish? In a river, perhaps, a lake, canal or even the sea. You must take into account how polluted the water is wherever you intend to start angling. A large river like the Thames carries a lot of sewage and chemicals. Fish from this sort of river don't taste very good, unless you go to the trouble of cultivating them in your bath for a week. But whether your parents would go along with that is another question!

You need different fishing or angling gear for different fishing grounds. To begin with the simplest equipment is best.

Three types of net and where to use them

With net A you catch crabs or small fish on sandy ground during a low tide.

Net B is used to catch fish living between rocks or in rock caves.

And net C is used to catch fish from a quay or river bank.

The bait is a fish head. Fasten it to the net, preferably with wooden sticks. Let the net down into the water until it touches the ground. Then lift it up again about 30cm high. Fasten the handle somewhere on the bank or quay. And if you think there might be fish in it pull it up carefully.

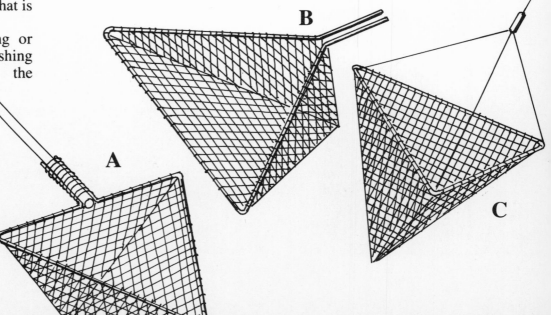

A

B

C

You need weights for angling

Weights keep the angling hook with the bait under water. You need round weights for fishing in running water or in waters with tides.

To catch fish from the river or sea-bed use flat or anchor-like weights.

These weights cost nothing

(Because they can be found anywhere, even in a tool box.)

lead nut

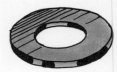

metal washer

stone with a hole

strips of lead

gunshot

These weights can be bought

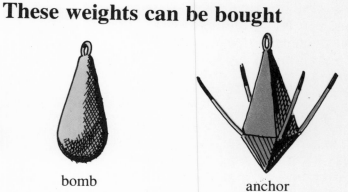

torpedo

bomb

anchor

When do you need a float?

If you want to catch fish that don't feed on the bottom of rivers or lakes you need floats. When the float disappears beneath the water a fish has swallowed the bait.

These floats can be bought

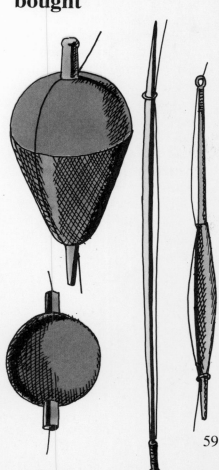

These floats cost nothing

The quill

Find yourself a bird's feather and rub off the feathery part. Fasten the quill to the line. Elastic bands are useful. The quill is effective in still waters.

The cigar tube

Fasten to the line with elastic bands. Useful for deep-sea fishing.

Brief guide to bait

Bait for freshwater fish

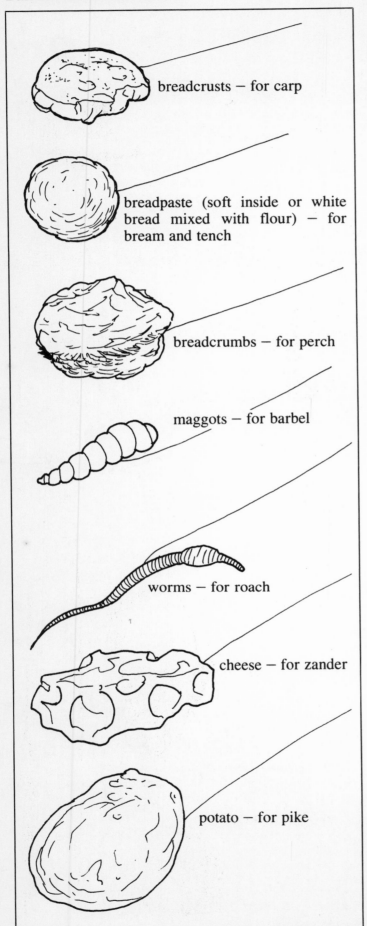

breadcrusts — for carp

breadpaste (soft inside or white bread mixed with flour) — for bream and tench

breadcrumbs — for perch

maggots — for barbel

worms — for roach

cheese — for zander

potato — for pike

Bait for saltwater fish

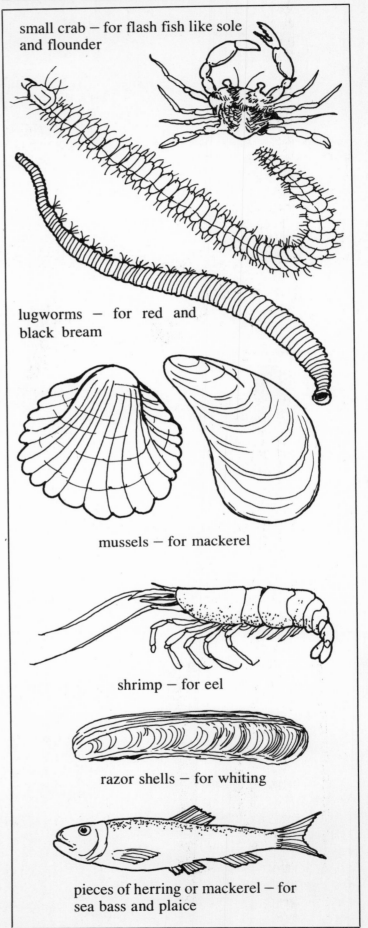

small crab — for flash fish like sole and flounder

lugworms — for red and black bream

mussels — for mackerel

shrimp — for eel

razor shells — for whiting

pieces of herring or mackerel — for sea bass and plaice

How your fishing tackle could look

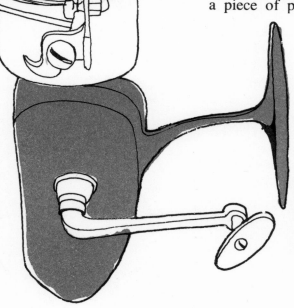

To begin with you don't need a proper fishing rod. Use a stick with a piece of string tied to it and fasten a hook and the bait at the other end. For a little money you can buy fishing line with a hook rolled onto a piece of plastic. And you can make a simple fishing reel yourself — with an empty cotton reel. And once you decide you really like fishing perhaps you could ask somebody for a real fishing rod as a present, like the one in the illustration.

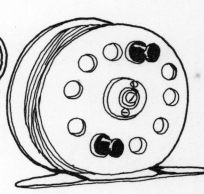

Tips

Learn the art of fishing by watching and asking experienced angling people. They will be pleased to help you.

And you can always ask for advice in a fishing tackle shop. But you should explain from the beginning that you don't have much money.

Casting the line

Standing on a bank, if your fishing rod is quite light, simply throw it over your head.

If there are trees or shrubs in the way throw it from the side. And when there is lots of space practice this mighty throw. That's the right way for angling from a quay or jetty.

Be an indoor gardener

How beautiful the world is when the plants begin to flower again in the spring. Trees put on their green robes, flowers display their lovely petals and the strong scent of fresh grass and flowers hangs over the land.

It is lovely to bring cut flowers indoors, to arrange them in vases and enjoy their fragrance and beauty. But after three or four days they will wilt and are over.

It seems a shame to strip the garden of flowers for the house. They will last so much longer in the garden and go on giving pleasure to everyone who passes or visits.

If you like to have flowers and plants indoors, or if you live in a flat and haven't got a garden, you can convert your room into an indoor garden.

That's what this chapter is all about. But first a few important things. You'll need compost and fertiliser for your garden; both can be bought in flower shops and garden centres. You need fertiliser when your plant has used up all the nutrients in the compost. And flowers and plants need water from which they also get nutrients.

It is important to water correctly. Test the soil with your fingers, if it sticks to your fingers it's damp enough. Otherwise you must give water. And place your plants on a saucer to prevent the water from running everywhere.

Branches

If a shrub is covered with lovely flowers you can carefully cut off a small branch, but don't damage the other branches. Place the branch in a tall vase or bottle and fill it with water. If you cut the stem at a slant at the bottom it can take up more water and will keep longer.

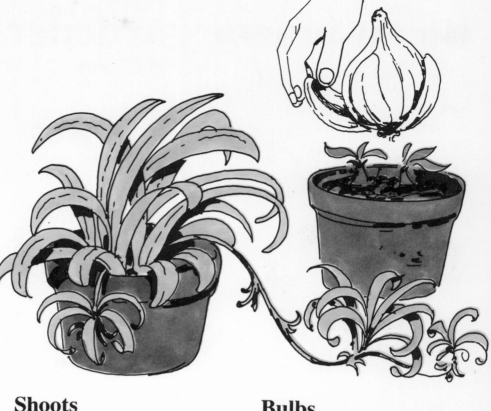

Shoots

Some plants form their own young plantlets by giving new shoots, like the spider plant for example. Cut off the strongest young plantlets or shoots and put them in a glass of water and new roots will soon form. Then plant them in a pot. Some plants can even form new shoots from their leaves, like the African Violet. Break off a leaf and stick it in the soil. It'll soon grow.

Bulbs

Many plants develop from bulbs. Of course, you can buy these in a garden shop. But you could carefully break off the little baby bulbs from tulip or daffodil bulbs and plant them yourself. New plants will grow from them.

Orange pips

You can grow little trees from the pips of oranges, lemons and tangerines. Take three or four pips from the fruit and press them gently into the well dampened compost. Then leave them in a warm, dark place. You have to leave them there for a few weeks, making sure the compost is kept moist.

Then place the pot on a sunny windowsill. As soon as the plant has two pairs of leaves transfer it to a bigger pot. After a few months — you will need patience — you will have little trees with dark shiny leaves. They flower and sometimes even have tiny fruit.

Miniature garden in a tray

You can construct a miniature garden in a shallow plastic tray. In addition to your tray you'll need potting compost, tiny plants and small pebbles or gravel.

Spread a layer of gravel over the bottom of the tray; this gives good drainage so the roots won't rot.

Now fill the tray with potting compost and water it well until the compost is really damp.

Set tiny plants into the compost with your fingertips and gently firm them in. Cover seeds with a thin layer of compost.

Carefully plant the roots into the compost. If they are too long spread them out a bit. Cover the stem and roots with compost.

Spray your miniature garden every day with a plant spray or mister.

You can place the little garden outside in the summer or put it on the windowsill.

A bottle garden

Our second suggestion is a garden made from glass. You will need a large big-bellied bottle and a few homemade tools like those in our illustration below.

A great advantage of a bottle garden is that it doesn't require much looking after once it is planted. If you seal the bottle with a cork you won't even have to water it very often.

To begin with you must thoroughly dry the bottle, perhaps with a hairdryer. On the bottom place a layer of charcoal, then fill it

Bottle tools

Fasten a fork, a spoon, a cotton reel and three or four pins to bamboo sticks. You also need a little sponge which you fasten to some flexible wire, and two thin sticks.

up to a third with potting compost.

With a spoon-spade dig holes for the little plants. With the cotton reel you gently press them in place after planting. Spread plants around evenly so they have plenty of space to grow. Climbers need a lot of space!

Planting is done with a little stick. Afterwards spray lukewarm water over the plants until the soil is quite moist. Then clean the inner walls of the bottle with the little sponge on a stick. Finally press in the cork. Don't place the bottle in direct sunlight but put it in a light place. If some plants become too tall carefully take them out and replace them with new young shoots.

You can plant African Violets, ferns and lilies in your bottle garden, but why won't you ask a florist or a gardener about the best plants to use.

Window boxes – not just for windows

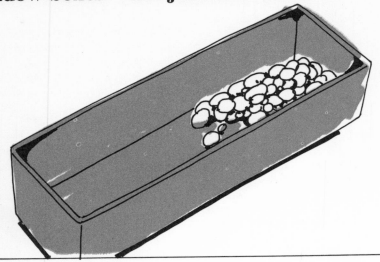

You don't have to put window boxes outside windows. Plants will also grow well in window boxes when placed in your room, provided you treat them properly.

You can buy window boxes made from plastic. Or you can make your own from wood but don't drill drainage holes in the bottom. Again, cover the bottom with a layer of gravel, covering the drainage holes with larger stones. Sprinkle with charcoal and then top up with potting compost or peat.

You can use those bulbs which you planted in the autumn so they can flower in the spring. You don't have to plant only flowering plants but also some evergreens so you will still have a nice looking window box when the flowers have gone.

When all the green plants die down for the winter you can decorate your box with evergreen branches of holly, ivy or fir.

A basket full of flowers

You can construct a hanging garden for the summer. Hang your basket full of flowers by your front door or from the ceiling in your room.

You need a wire or plastic basket and some chain to hang it up with. You can work better with your basket if you place it on a bucket.

Line the bottom of the basket with a layer of fresh moss, then a layer of peat. That will keep the moisture in the soil. Fill up the basket with potting compost again. Make a hollow in the centre to store the water.

Now you can put in the plants, the largest ones in the middle of the smaller, trailing plants around the edge. The big picture on the right illustrates which plants are specially suitable for your hanging basket.

Once you've planted everything dip the entire basket into a bath full of water so the soil can be thoroughly saturated. When the soil has dried up again repeat the bath.

Good plants for your hanging garden are **creeping jenny**, the tall, upright and bright **geraniums**, **petunias** that flower all summer long. Around the edge you can have **nasturtiums** and there are several kinds of trailing **fuchsias**. The different types of **begonias** also look very pretty. And don't forget the lovely deep blue of the **lobelias**.

Your own garden bed

If you have a garden at home you could create your own little garden.

Start in the spring. Take a spade and dig over the soil. You should dig as deep as the blade of your spade and don't tread on the dug soil.

After digging you can separate the area into beds. One bed should be about 1.2m wide. Make a path about 30cm wide between the beds which you can firm down with your feet. Now the beds must be carefully raked until you have an even, light, crumbly layer of soil.

Sowing

Sowing is not that easy. First make some drills about a hand width apart. They should be about 2.5cm deep.

Sow very thinly. Label the bed with the name of your plants or with the bag the seeds came in. Then lightly cover the seeds with soil, using the rake. Press down the soil gently. Next day you can water the bed carefully. As soon as the first young shoots appear you can start cultivating and weeding.

What you can plant

Strawberries, lettuce, cabbage and tomatoes. You can buy these plants from the garden centre.

The distance between the plants depends on the size of the grown plant. Never plant too closely. A lettuce needs at least 25cm to grow properly.

And remember that young plants need plenty of water, the beds must be tidied and weeded regularly for your plants to grow well. Regularly means at least once a week. Raking is very important for the root growth of weeds takes up important growing space — they must be removed.

What grows in one summer?

Poppies, nasturtiums, marigolds and fuchsias. If you want your garden to flower in the spring you must plant some bulbs in the autumn. Plant these about 6cm deep.

Spring flowers are: tulips, daffodils, hyacinths and crocuses. You can also buy autumn-flowering bulbs. These must be planted in the spring. These are dahlias or gladioli. You can take out the bulbs after they have flowered in the autumn and overwinter them in a frost-free room.

Tips

Watch out for slugs; they usually emerge after rain.

Even the best soil needs some fertiliser eventually. The best fertiliser is from a compost heap where all organic waste, like dead plants and vegetables, return to become good soil.

There is also the mild humus fertiliser or manure.

Surveillance, investigations, hiding, disguise

—A detective must be versatile

There are spies among us! Detectives and secret agents everywhere . . . aren't there? If you know all about 'agentology' you won't only spend hours observing, discovering and reconnoitering — you'll also be communicating with your friends and conspirators without being found out by others.

We would like to introduce you to the art of being a secret agent, because it's fun and through it one can learn a lot. Playing detective sharpens the wits, improves the powers of concentration and teaches one to think clearly and act quickly.

So how good a secret agent are you? We have depicted here several detectives doing their work. Try to find out who is observing whom, and with what.

Well, what have you found out? How would you go about disguising yourself or taking up a watch position as unobtrusively as possible?

69

Letter-boxes, hiding places, disguises and invisible inks . . .

In this picture you see various kinds of secret letter-boxes or 'dead waiters'. Here secret agents habitually make their 'drops' for the couriers. The couriers transport the information to the boss at headquarters who then evaluates it.

Try to find all the hidden letter-boxes in the picture; if you can do that, you should be able to find your opponent's information and start to 'crack' their secret code.

Spies are often 'on the run'. How can they hide or get rid of pursuers? Change buses, run through crowded pedestrian zones and department stores, run up going-down escalators, change lifts .. . . Of course, you know all about this.

An agent needs many hiding places and disguises if he doesn't want to be discovered straight away. An empty teabag stuck to the inside of your coat sleeve is a good place for a secret message. You can be sure, even when searched,

that your hidden message will be safe.

To hide messages in your shoe cut out two false soles from cardboard. Make sure the careboard sole fits comfortably in your shoes, then with sticky tape fasten the piece of paper containing your message to the underside of the sole.

Potato ink

Cut a potato in half and squeeze the juice into a basin. With a sharp wooden stick dipped in the juice write your message on paper. On drying the writing becomes invisible, but readable again when pressed with a hot iron or placed in a hot oven.

Water ink

Soak a sheet of paper thoroughly in water and lay it flat onto a smooth surface. Cover it with a dry sheet on which you write your message. Hold the wet paper against the light and it is visible. The writing disappears when the paper dries. But when wet it's visible again.

Wax ink

Rub a sheet of paper with a white candle. Turn it over and place another sheet underneath. Write on the top, the wax will mark the sheet underneath. If the receiver sprinkles it with coloured powder (such as coffee) and then shakes off the surplus, the powder will stick to the writing.

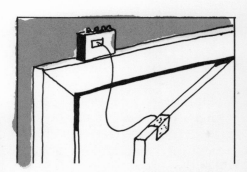

Disguise

You can disguise yourself by simple means. Use different kinds of headgear, hats, spectacles, false beards and moustaches. A towel is a useful device; roll it into a sausage shape and place it inside your jacket. You now have wide, impressive shoulders. You can put an arm in a sling. You can tie a cushion to your stomach. But remember: you must also alter the way you move.

Camouflage

You can alter your appearance – with a wig, a different parting, with hair gel, or a set of false teeth. Change your face with false eyebrows, by painting it with wrinkles or stuffing your cheeks with cotton wool balls to make it

look fatter. If you want to be professional, dye your hair (with talcum powder or washout spray colours). Stick on a false nose, wear a large coat, a hat pulled over your eyes and dark glasses.

Traps

Set traps for other agents. Glue a thin thread across a corridor, stick a hair between the door and the door frame. Place several sheets of paper on a table and mark two sheets with a thin line. You can check whether the line is still correct. Make a sound trap: seal one side of a match-box and fill it with peas. Place it on top of the door frame. Glue a piece of thin thread to the box and the other end to the door!

A secret agent must know all the

The most important rule for the secret agent is that he knows about all the different secret codes, how they are spoken, read and coded.

There are numerous different coding systems. Every day the secret services of most countries work at decoding and translating messages.

But let's begin with the obvious, when two agents want to communicate with each other across a distance they use semaphore. Each arm position represents a letter. Here are the letters of the semaphore alphabet!

Written code 1: Insert an A after every two letters; start after the first letter.

YAOU AWEARE AFOALLAOWAED

Written code 2: Insert an A after the first letter; then a B after two letters and then after every letter one further in the alphabet (that's C . . D . . .).

YAOBU WCEDREE FFGOHLILJOKWLEMD

Written code 3: Reverse the letters of each word.

UOY EREW DEWOLLOF

Written code 4: Write your message in groups of two letters each.

YO UW ER E F OL LL OW ED

Written code 5: Deduct one letter from each letter.
Y minus 1 equals X for example

XNT VDQD ENKKNVDC

72

codes

and shapes as well as dots, clock faces, winking with the eyelids and many other devices for your secret codes.

The written codes, too, which we have shown you, can be developed further for your own needs, for example using numbers as a basis, or re-arranging letter groups . . . We won't tell you any more!

The illustration on the left shows a slide rule for codes. It works like this: each message begins with a cover word whose first letter shows which code is in use for the message. If it is a small letter h, for example, the rule is adjusted to that and the message reads like this: 1Kgn, QK Qrn NbBnN. That means: come to the river!

We have illustrated, on the right, another alphabet. If you want to communicate without speaking you can do so with the help of the finger language or sign language. But this type of talking is only advisable if both of you have mastered the finger alphabet without making mistakes. The sender must be able to 'write' the words as well as the receiver can translate them. Therefore you must really practice before using it for real.

You should really try and invent your own codes, and be able to understand your messages! Here are a few tips: you can use colours

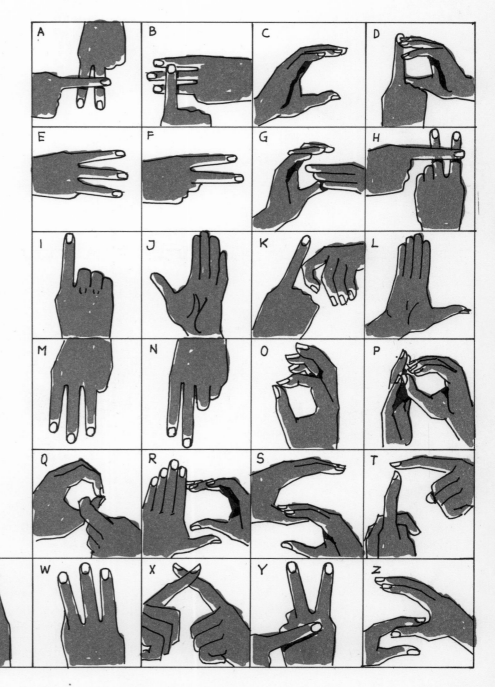

73

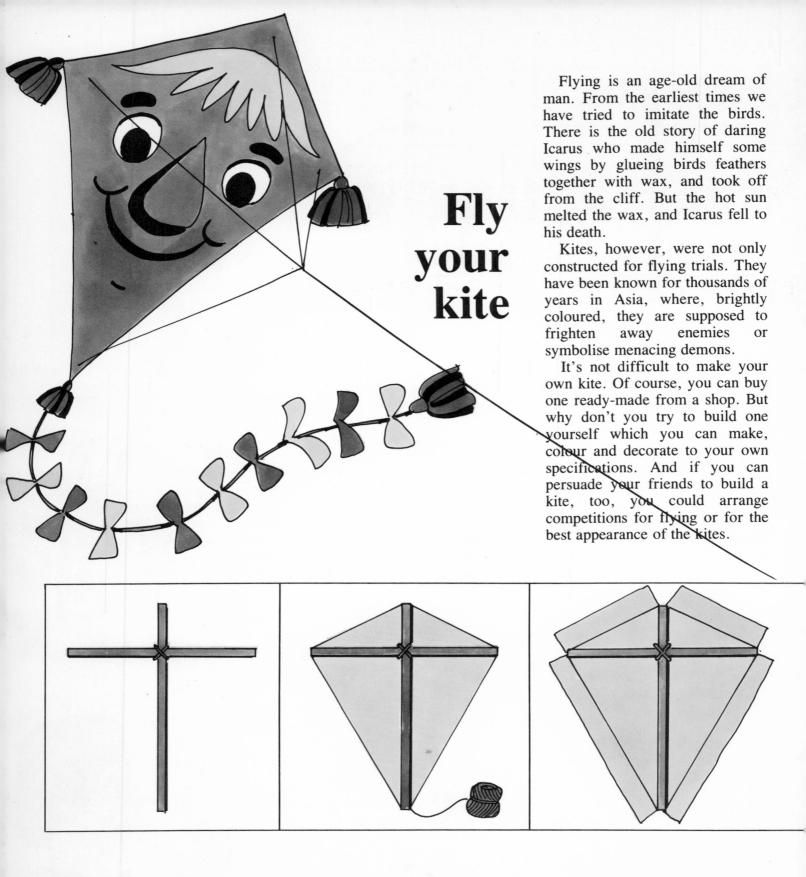

Fly your kite

Flying is an age-old dream of man. From the earliest times we have tried to imitate the birds. There is the old story of daring Icarus who made himself some wings by glueing birds feathers together with wax, and took off from the cliff. But the hot sun melted the wax, and Icarus fell to his death.

Kites, however, were not only constructed for flying trials. They have been known for thousands of years in Asia, where, brightly coloured, they are supposed to frighten away enemies or symbolise menacing demons.

It's not difficult to make your own kite. Of course, you can buy one ready-made from a shop. But why don't you try to build one yourself which you can make, colour and decorate to your own specifications. And if you can persuade your friends to build a kite, too, you could arrange competitions for flying or for the best appearance of the kites.

The pointed kite

Here we show you two basic shapes for a kite and how they are built. But there are many more shapes you could make, like a hexagonal kite or a box kite. For the basic shape connect two wooden battens together, one about 50cm long and one 25cm long, both about 5×10mm thick.

Where they should cross is shown on the diagram. You can tie the battens together with string.

Cut a notch in each end of the sticks. Insert a piece of thin, strong cord into the notches and pull tight. Now you have the skeleton for your kite.

Now lay a sheet of paper (parchment is best) beneath the frame and cut out an area that should overhang the edges by about 10cm all round. Cut into the corners and brush all edges with glue. Fold over the paper and wrap it round the taut string.

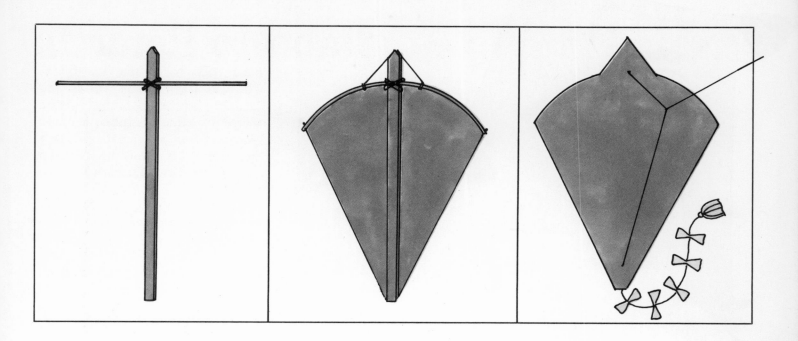

The bow kite

The bow kite has better flying qualities than the pointed kite as you'll soon find out. You need a batten about 1m long and 12×8mm thick, and also a piece of dowelling about 85 cm long and 1cm thick.

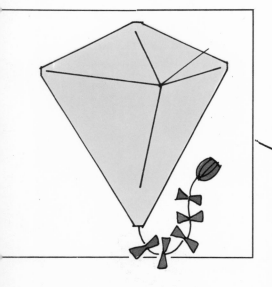

Now fix what is called the balance. That is string tied to the ends of each of the four points of the frame, about 10cm away. Now place your finger underneath the string and let the kite hang down. Move the string until the kite hangs perfectly level.

Attach a tail with coloured bows of paper and your kite is ready.

Now, like the pointed kite, cut out a large piece of parchment and fasten it to the frame. Fix a balance and even out the kite. You can adjust it a bit by trying out different lengths of tail.

Cut a notch into the ends of the batten and dowelling. Tie or glue the stick to the batten about 10cm from the top.

Ready to fly

You now need some 100 to 200m of strong cord on a roll. Let out about 1m of cord and take the kite in one hand and the roll in the other. Position yourself against the wind, preferably on an incline, and run. Throw the kite into the air. Run quickly, feeding out the cord until the kite is high up. You'll probably have to practice the start several times. But you'll be pleased once your kite is flying high in the air.

One more thing: never let your kite fly near power cables or airfields.

Now stretch a piece of cord from one end of the dowelling stick across the bottom of the batten and to the other end of the stick. Above the kite stretch a short length of cord across the top of the batten as shown in the picture.

From Maja in Findland to Peter in

There is nothing better than a good, loyal friendship. Friends who are inseparable, go through thick and thin together. And it's really sad when one's best friend moves to a different place.

But it doesn't have to be like that. The post office works at making communication possible between people who live far apart. Not just over the telephone but also through postcards, letters, telegrams, parcels and packets. The post is a clever institution (though we sometimes get annoyed if a letter arrives too late or is even lost).

You probably write a postcard to your grandmother when you are on holiday. Well, then you should be able to communicate with your friend in Newcastle or Cardiff.

The friendship between pen-friends can often span years or even decades. Whenever one of the friends has something on his mind he writes about it to the other — and receives ideas, advice and a sympathetic listener in return. Sharing problems is often the best remedy.

And what could you do if you met a nice Swedish girl or a Spanish boy while on holiday abroad? Well, you could write to each other. If you know a foreign language it makes it easier, of course, to communicate with a foreign friend.

But if you cannot or don't want to travel to far-away places why don't you let the big wide world come home to you, through the letter-box? You can find pen-friends through pen-friend clubs, youth magazines or embassies. And then you can start to write — about your home, your town, country, area, your friends and your brothers or sisters . . . That would all be interesting to your pen-friends. They might be living in Australia and have no idea of what Britain is like.

You can collect the replies and accounts, and even photographs, until your wall is covered with souvenirs from your friend's home.

Tunbridge Wells

Peter met the little Finnish girl, Maja, when he and his family were driving down to Italy for their holidays. They stopped next to a Finnish family at a lay-by on an Austrian motorway, and the two children soon became friends although they couldn't communicate too well. When they discovered that they were going to the same place in Italy they jumped up and down for joy.

They have been writing to each other for three years now. During the last summer Peter was invited to visit Maja's family in Jyväskylä. That's about 180 miles/300 kilometres north of the Finnish capital of Helsinki.

The journey there was great fun. First by train, then by a large ferry across the sea, and then a long drive through Finland. Then Peter saw for himself all the hundreds of lakes and islands of Maja's country which she had written about in her letters. It was a super holiday. And they still write to each other.

A letter chain

Obviously a pen-friendship only lasts as long as the friends continue writing to each other. To keep your interest going you could start a letter chain. For instance, try to find friends in five different countries, or even continents.

The first friend starts the chain by writing, say, two pages out of 10, listing all the things he wants to tell, and in a language that's understood by the others. He sends his letter to the second friend in the chain who tells his news on the next two pages. That letter goes to the third friend and so on until the letter is returned to the first person. You could change the person who starts the letter chain so that each friend can keep at least one chain letter.

All five friends could also write to each other at the same time. But that would be a lot of work and could become confusing.

Collecting friends

By writing to friends you have the best means of 'collecting' countries, too. Just imagine you had pen-friends in Italy, France, Germany and Luxembourg. Start by collecting everything you learn from your pen-friends, or otherwise, about these countries.

After a short time you'll find you can not only surprise your pen-friends with your knowledge of their country but your room, too, can change to an international landscape. You can compare your two countries and find out their differences in culture and habits. Or you could just collect the stamps!

From classroom to classroom

Perhaps you have heard of a letter friendship between classes. A school class in a town in Britain might write to a class in Germany, or an American class may keep in close contact with a class in France, by letter-writing.

Each week the class writes a long letter in English, German and/or French. And all the news

Keeping an autograph book

Roses are red,
Violets are blue,
Sugar is sweet
And so are you.

It used to be the custom among young girls to own an autograph book. They would invite their friends and acquaintances to write a poem, a verse or a worthy comment in the book. And perhaps they might add a dried flower or a similar token.

in the book. It could be a word of thanks for a nice evening, a few funny comments or praise for the cook.

Perhaps you might like to revive the old custom of keeping an autograph book. You needn't be idle yourself — you could add the date and author of each entry as well as a few thoughts you connect with it.

You can buy an autograph book — they are often beautifully bound and some can be locked so that only those with your permission can read it. But you could simply use an exercise book.

If you have a very good friend you could keep a book together. There are sometimes things one can't tell even to the best of friends but to write about them might be easier.

about the class; any problems, or the latest events in the town or country, local sport, television, films or pop music, all information is exchanged by way of letter.

The original idea of the autograph book has changed a little (see page 8). Adults have their own version of the autograph book — the visitors' book. Each visitor to the house is invited to write something

Day One: Friday, 8th September . . .

There are many people who keep a diary — in various shapes and sizes. The important thing is why one wants to keep a diary. Here are a few possibilities, but there are many more.

Personal diary

A good reason to start a diary is the beginning of a new friendship. Everything that happens to you and your friend, your thoughts about it, perhaps thoughts you wouldn't tell anybody else — all this can be taken down in your diary.

You can make a daily entry in your diary and have a continuous record of your life. You can read about the various events, find out whether you have changed at all, why, how and when.

Another possibility is to only write in your diary when something really important has happened to you. Or when you've got something on your mind but haven't got the right person to talk to.

various regions through which you travel, the people you meet during the course of the day. You can write about the events and discoveries you make. You needn't write in an elaborate style. Just the way the thoughts come into your head.

You could arrange your travel diary according to the days, or countries and places. Illustrate it by sticking in pictures and souvenirs like tickets and receipts, photos and postcards, stickers and suchlike. That way you can create an illustrated memento of your travels.

Some people always carry a little book with them in which they note every idea that comes into their head. This book could become valuable, too — when you don't know what present to give,

what to play, which books to read, where to go, etc. Why not try it?

Consider whether your diary is meant for others. If not, always lock it away.

Travel diary

You can create a valuable treasure by writing a diary of your travels during the holidays. You could describe the journey, the

How easily we can be fooled . . .

What would we do without our eyes? We would have no idea of colour, shape, things, the beauty of people and landscapes, the horror of accidents, war and destruction. Our eyes are an important part of our 'perception', the way in which we make sense of the world.

But our eyes can be easily deceived. As the sun goes down it looks much bigger, but when it stands high in the sky at noon it looks much smaller. The reason is that in the evening you see the sun near to the earth and can compare its size to houses and trees. It looks really huge, doesn't it?

Or try looking into a bowl of water in which an object is immersed. Depending on the angle you look into the bowl the object appears larger or smaller — or it disappears completely. Light is broken by water, it is *refracted*.

Everything connected with light and its effects belongs to the subject 'optics'. When the eye is tricked in some way it's called an optical illusion.

Here is a black square divided into 25 small squares. If you look at it for a little while you'll notice a 'dirty' shadow in the white space between four black squares. The point furthest away from the crossing of the white lines is surrounded by a larger area of black and appears lighter.

Our brain works pretty fast — but not as fast as the light. On the left and right you see two identical

drawings except that the one on the left is 'negative', that is white on a black background while the one on the right is 'positive', the reverse.

Look very hard at one of the drawings. Then look at a white wall. Can you see something? Yes, the drawing appears on the wall, not as clear but recognisable. You even see the picture when you don't look at it any more. Now see whether it works the same with the drawing on the right.

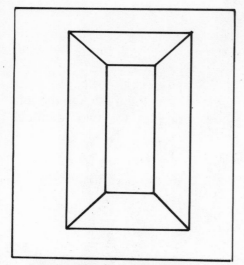

Look at the inner rectangle: does it move to the back or front when you look at it?

These two ladders aren't the same length, or are they? Is the one at the back twice as long?

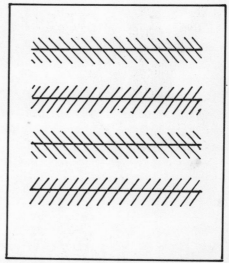

The four long lines crossing the slanting lines run parallel. Or do they?

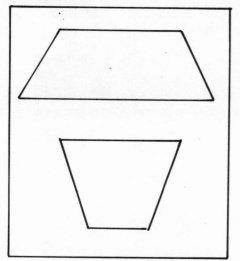

You see two trapeziums. Look at the top line of each of them. Which is longer?

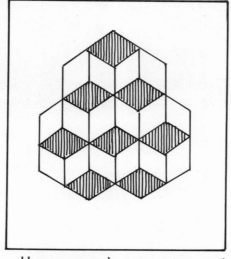

How many cubes can you count? Look at them again. Do they change?

This hat is about twice as high as it is wide. Or is it as wide as it is high?

Are the two horizontal lines curved, or exactly parallel?

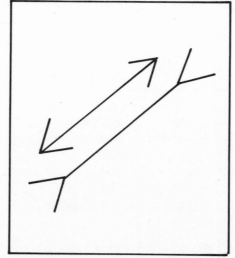

What do you think about the length of the two lines? Are they the same or is the lower one longer?

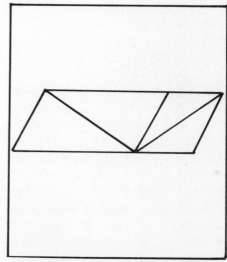

The left and right diagonals have something in common. What is it?

Pets need love and attention

Humans and animals

At the beginning of human history, before agriculture or industry were thought of, human beings regarded animals simply as a source of food and clothing; they were hunters. As nomads, they followed the great herds of animals so they always had access to their food source.

But one day, probably by accident, man discovered that it could be done differently by preventing the herds from wandering. They guarded the herds and drove them into fenced enclosures. Then the people found out that the animals could be used to work for them. Domesticated animals need food as they couldn't graze while wandering about. So agriculture developed, at first to provide food for the animals which in their turn provided food for the people. By pulling the plough or cart the animals more or less worked for their food.

Pets

During the course of time people learned more and more about nature and animals. They turned wild wolves into tame dogs, horses into trained mounts for riding . . .

But the children didn't just look at animals as a source of meat, milk and clothing. They played with the young animals. They caught small creatures and took them home just as they do today. That's how we came to have pets.

If you want to have a pet of your own, don't just take any animal. You should first take into consideration those animals you like and dislike, of which you are afraid, the habitat the animal prefers and whether you can provide the right conditions. If you are thinking of a dog, for example, do you know how much exercise it needs and whether it can live in a small home? Ask friends and neighbours about their pets and what problems they have with them. In short, prepare yourself for your pet.

Pets for your room

Where to get them from

Once you have decided on a pet where do you get it from? Pet shops offer a wide variety of animals. But why don't you find out about other places too? Go along to the nearest animal rescue centre. You'll see many beautiful and lovable animals there which once belonged to someone but which have been abandoned by their owners because they were too much trouble.

Why not help one of these creatures? You'll find animal-loving people in the rescue centres who know how to look after animals. Talk to the experts, they can give you a lot of advice. You might learn from them how best to handle a pet so it isn't afraid of you; how to feed it and care for it, how to help it when it is ill.

You could also talk to a game-keeper in the forest who could tell you a lot about the animals there. You never know, you might hear about a poor little creature that has been found abandoned some-where.

Now, let's be a bit more specific. On the next pages you can find out what guinea pigs like, what cats hate, what fish eat and what birds drink. Have fun with your pet. And remember, above all it needs love.

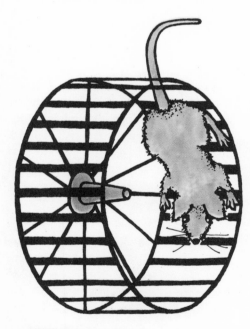

White mice

For preference take two young white mice from the same litter. If they are related they'll get on better. But remember that if you choose a male and a female then you'll soon have many little ones. That is alright if you know that friends or a local pet shop will be

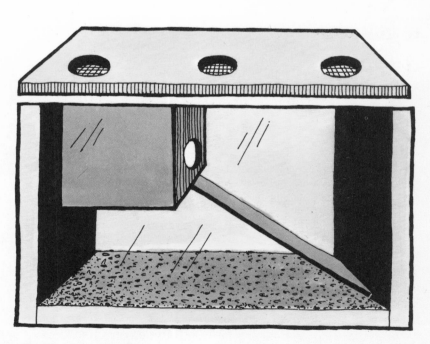

able to find homes for them.

Your white mice will need a cage. If you put in some bits of paper or rags they will make themselves a nest to sleep in. Try to make them a climbing toy, a ladder or frame, and a wheel if

possible, so they don't get bored.

They eat hard bread, various grains, a little greenery and sometimes a little minced meat. They must have a constant supply of water in a special drinking bottle.

The hamster

A hamster will need a larger cage – and warmth. Make him a box for sleeping within the cage, he'll make his own nest from bits of paper and rags. He likes to be comfortable.

Your hamster not only eats grains – he hoards them, too. First in his big cheeks, then in his box where he digs them in to store for bad times – in case you forget to feed him!

The hamster is a clean animal – he preens himself like a cat. You must clean out his cage every day so he is really comfortable.

He sleeps during the day – he is a noctural creature. But you can still play with him – just before bedtime. Close your bedroom door and let him run free about the room. Watch out that he doesn't run up the curtains. That could be trouble as a hamster can very swiftly tear out bits of the curtain and hide them in his cheeks! In its natural habitat a hamster will

hibernate (winter sleep). However, if it is kept in a warm place the hamster probably will not hibernate.

The guinea pig

A guinea pig needs a large cage. You can make a sleeping box for him, too. If you have a garden he will like it there. His cage should look like a play-pen.

The sleeping box should be a little house which gives protection against rain and cold. The best bedding is a layer of hay for your pet.

Guinea pigs like to eat greenery, root vegetables, corn, hard bread, cooked rice and cooked potatoes – they eat almost anything. And a lot, too: up to 250g a day.

The cage must be very, very clean as it soon smells badly otherwise.

Your first aquarium

It is always interesting to watch fish swimming about in an aquarium. When starting an aquarium begin with a small one. Once your parents see you taking care of it you might get a bigger one soon enough.

Start with a cold water aquarium for fresh water fish, as a heating system will be rather expensive.

You need to plant some aquatic plants such as pond weed. Sprinkle the bottom of the aquarium with fine sand and arrange the plants in it. Add a few pebbles.

The water has to be poured in very carefully so as not to disturb the plants. It's best to use distilled water which is available from chemists. Add about a quarter teaspoon of salt to every 10 litres of water.

Wait a few days until the plants have acclimatised themselves before you put in the fish. Don't forget an air pump as the fish must be able to breathe properly.

Have only a few fish to begin with and remember that not all fish get on with each other. Goldfish and comet fish, for example, get on well together.

Feed your fish with live or dried food. Dried food can be bought in pet shops, live food like water-flies and earth-worms can be found anywhere.

The vivarium

Whether a dry or a bog vivarium, it must be big enough. You can make your own by building a wooden frame. Three sides and the top are covered with fine wire mesh and one side has a pane of glass. That's a dry vivarium. A bog vivarium should have a glass wall at least 10 cm high all round.

Cover the bottom of your dry vivarium with a 5 cm layer of sand and in one corner arrange some peat mixed with moss. Some creatures like to hide themselves so provide some sort of hiding place made from stones. Climbing creatures need a branch or some twigs.

For a bog vivarium cover the bottom with plenty of peat and moss. In addition, plant a few grasses and don't forget a little pond. Make a border of pebbles around it and place a bigger stone in the middle. You must spray your vivarium daily with water.

You can collect some animals from the wild during the spring and keep them in your vivarium. In the winter you must return them to the wild.

Feed your animals regularly and give them plenty to drink. Most eat

insects. A tortoise also likes grass, fruit, herbs and lettuce. It hibernates from the beginning of October. Put it in a box filled with leaves, moss and twigs and keep it in a cool, dark place. Before hibernation give your tortoise a bath with lukewarm water; that induces it to empty its stomach and intestines which need to be completely empty during hibernation.

Your tortoise will wake again at the beginning of March. Wash it again with lukewarm water before you return it to the vivarium and feed it.

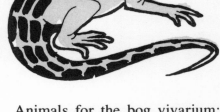

Animals for the bog vivarium: toads, salamanders, newts.

Animals for the dry vivarium: frogs, small tortoises.

Caring for cats

There are many types of cats; the most popular are the Siamese, the Persian, the Angora and the common house cat.

Special breeds are expensive but house cats are not, and you might be given a kitten. Chose a kitten from a litter where you know the mother and you are sure it has been well cared for. But leave your kitten at least six weeks, better still eight weeks with its mother.

Your kitten will need a soft little basket or a softly cushioned box, a tray filled with cat litter — and a name. Call it by its name as often as possible so it gets to know it quickly. If you keep the cat litter clean you will have a clean cat.

Cats have their own personality but if you give them a lot of attention, play and talk with them and feed them they become very attached to you and not at all shy. Never hit a cat. If it has been naughty be really cross with it or slap it gently with a newspaper. Don't disturb your cat when it's asleep. You can play with it when it's awake and lively.

Don't leave your cat alone for a long time. You can leave it for a weekend if you leave enough food and drink, but not any longer. In that case you have to find someone who will look after it. Try to find somebody who also has a cat so you can take turns in looking after each other's cat.

You can get your cat used to eating left-over scraps of meat as well as cat food. If you give your cat dry food, which is good for its teeth, make sure it has a bowl of water, too.

Dogs are loyal friends

Man recognised very early on the value of the dog. At first as a partner for hunting and for guard duties, later as a playmate and companion.

A great variety of dogs have been developed through selective breeding, but they are all descendants of the wolf.

There is no other animal that appears in as many different shapes and sizes as the dog. If you look at the difference between a huge St. Bernhard and a tiny chihuahua you can see the extent of the development over about 10,000 years.

Dogs are carnivores. They like to eat meat like tripe, liver and other offal. But bones, too, are important for them, not so much for nourishment but more for keeping their teeth clean.

A dog needs a lot of exercise, it shouldn't be locked up in a tiny flat. If you keep a dog in a city flat you must make sure you take your dog out a lot. Make it run and play with you.

The world of the dog consists mainly of scents. That's why it likes to sniff at you and everything else. Dogs can't see long distances very well. Some scientists believe that they can only see in black and white. So, dogs rely on their sense of smell which is very well developed.

Perhaps you can understand, now, why dogs are always cocking their legs and leaving a sample of their scent. They mark their territory with scent, like an invisible fence.

If you closely observe your dog you'll find it really interesting. You can learn a lot from the way dogs behave towards each other. Try to 'read' the face of your dog and discover its moods. And never abuse its loyalty.

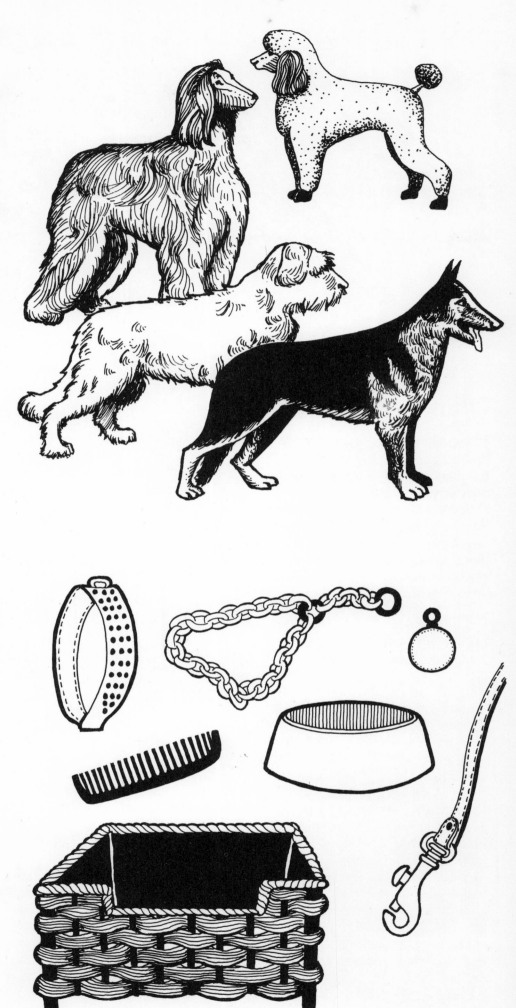

Birds

To be honest no bird should ever be shut in a cage. Birds love their freedom as much as any other animal — and a bird that was born to fly should be allowed to fly and not be locked in a cage. But talking about pets there are exceptions. Since long, long ago people have enjoyed the company of song birds. They caught them, tamed and bred them.

Some species could not now survive outside captivity. They wouldn't know how to feed themselves nor how to protect themselves in the daily battle against natural enemies. So, you can rest assured that the birds you keep at home in cages don't mind at all as long as they are properly cared for. These birds are mainly canaries, budgerigars and finches. Parrots, too, are quite happy in a large enough cage. You may, too, give them the opportunity to fly about inside the house.

You should easily be able to make or buy a suitable cage for your bird. The cage must be kept clean. A removable bottom tray is useful here. In addition the feeding and watering arrangements must be accessible from the outside. Never buy a cage that is smaller than $60 \times 50 \times 40$ cm.

Make it comfortable for your feathered friend. There's always enough space for a few twigs, some sand and pebbles in the cage. And your bird will really enjoy a perch or a swing and a mirror.

The canary

Without doubt this one is the opera star among the birds; not many others equal its voice. And the canary doesn't need much looking after, either. Special canary food is available, and you can provide plenty of greenery like watercress, fresh lettuce and so on. Obviously they need a continuous supply of fresh water, too. Canaries like to bathe frequently, so provide enough water for that, but make sure the water isn't ice-cold. The cage must be cleaned about once a week.

The budgerigar

The canary is a beautiful bright yellow colour, but the budgie comes in many colours, mainly blues and greens. Even more fun than the canary's singing, a budgie, if properly trained, can learn to talk. Not as well as a parrot, perhaps, but it might learn to say your name or its own without too much difficulty.

Feeding is the same as for the canary. But it needs to be occupied most of the time — a budgie can feel very lonely. So talk and play with it. It likes to fly about the room, but take care it doesn't escape through an open window. It will probably not find its way back, and cannot survive for long outside.

Finches

Finches need the least space; they live happily with each other so you can have several in one cage. But don't put one of the native finches in your cage, they are used to freedom and might perish. Pet finches come from Australia and Africa. They feed on grains but also need some greenery from time to time. And they must always have a supply of fresh water.

Even great chefs started small

We not only eat because we are hungry but also because we enjoy our food. Some adults get very excited over the name of a famous chef.

But even these chefs weren't born great cooks. So just have a go and start. Ask an adult for advice. Then go shopping for the ingredients of the dish you want to cook. But only buy what you've noted on your shopping list. It's all too easy to get carried away in those big enticing supermarkets and you end up with a lot of nice but unnecessary things which cost too much.

Brief cooking guide

Although we tried to keep this chapter quite simple there are some special cooking terms which you might find in a cookery book and can't quite understand. Here is a brief explanation of the most common terms.

thicken
Means to blend soups and sauces with a thickener like egg yolk, flour and butter, cream or cornflour to make it less runny.

blanch
Means immersing meat or vegetables briefly in boiling water to improve flavour or appearance.

brown
Means frying, onions for example, until they turn brown, and baking or grilling dishes until the top colours.

steam
Cooking food in its own steam, or the steam from water.

reduce
Means cooking (boiling) sauces continuously until they have become quite thick.

stock
Is the cooking liquid from meat or vegetables.

deep-fry
Means cooking food in a deep pan of oil or fat (sticks of potato become chips).

cook
Means turning something raw into something soft and edible.

au gratin
A dish covered with cheese and/or breadcrumbs and browned in the oven or under the grill.

saute
Means frying lightly or quickly.

coat
Means covering food with egg and breadcrumbs or batter before frying.

sieve
Means rubbing food through a sieve or strainer to remove any coarse parts.

puree
Food mashed or liquidised to a pulp and sometimes passed through a sieve.

swell
Rice is cooked until swollen. Bring twice as much water as rice to the boil, cook uncovered at first, then cover with a lid and leave over a low heat until the rice is cooked and all the water is used up.

stew
Cooking with a little liquid until tender.

bouquet garni
Means a selection of fresh or dried herbs added to the food during cooking for added flavour.

Vitamins are important nutrients

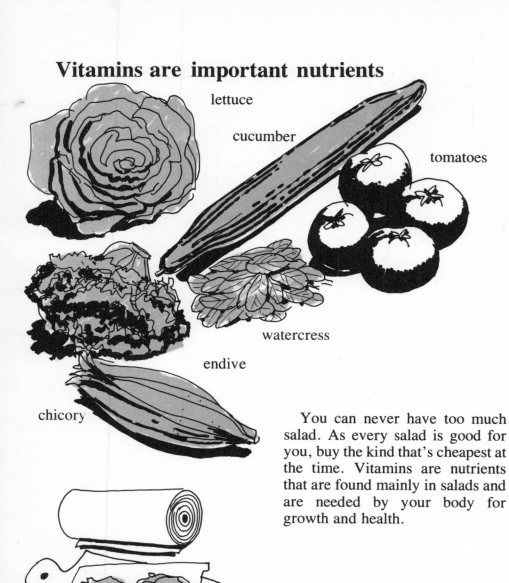

lettuce

cucumber

tomatoes

watercress

endive

chicory

You can never have too much salad. As every salad is good for you, buy the kind that's cheapest at the time. Vitamins are nutrients that are found mainly in salads and are needed by your body for growth and health.

Salad tips

After washing, dry the salad carefully before tossing it in salad dressing.

Immerse endive and chicory in warm water for a little while and they won't be bitter.

Onions improve the flavour of any salad. Try adding slices of apple or orange to a chicory salad.

A small tin of tuna fish turns a plain salad into something special. Salad makes a good starter to a meal as well as a tasty accompaniment.

Salad dressings

Oil-and-vinegar dressing or vinaigrette

Blend about 2×15ml spoons of vinegar with salt, pepper and a little mustard. With a whisk beat in about 4×15ml spoons of oil, drop by drop.

You can add a little garlic to this sauce to make it really nice. Finely chop the clove of garlic or crush it in a garlic press.

This dressing goes very well with lettuce, endive, tomato or mixed salad.

Cream dressing

Blend about 4×15ml spoons of single (light) cream with a little lemon juice, salt, pepper and dill. Very good with cucumber salad.

Yogurt-herb dressing

Blend a pot of low-fat yogurt with a little mayonnaise. Season with salt, pepper, thyme and basil. This sauce goes well with chicory.

Tasty egg dishes

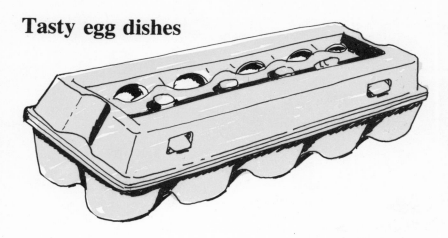

Scrambled eggs with bacon and onions

For each person you need:
2 eggs
2 slices of streaky bacon
1 small onion, salt and pepper

Beat the eggs with salt and pepper in a bowl. Chop the bacon and onions until very small. First fry the bacon in a frying pan. When it is brown add the onions. As soon as they are transparent pour in the eggs and stir with a wooden spoon until they are set.

Super eggs on toast

For each person you need:
2 eggs
1 large slice of bread, toasted
curry powder, paprika powder, salt and pepper

Heat a little oil in a frying pan. Carefully break in two eggs and fry them until the egg white is set. Place the eggs on the toast and sprinkle the lot with a little curry and paprika powder, salt and pepper.

Fried potatoes with a difference

For four people you need:
about 1kg of potatoes
2 large onions
2×5ml spoons caraway and 2×5ml spoons rosemary
salt and pepper

Peel the potatoes and cut them into small pieces. Fry the sliced onions in plenty of oil and add the potatoes and flavourings. After 25 minutes the dish will be ready.

Mushroom omelette

For four people you need:
12 eggs
1 small tin of button mushrooms
butter
salt, pepper, garlic
(you can use fresh mushrooms but you must trim them first)

Cut the mushrooms into thin slices and cook them in a little butter. Then pour in the egg mixture (made as with scrambled eggs) and cook the omelette until set.

Spinach bake

For four people you need:
2×250g packets of frozen spinach
5 eggs
½ pot single (light) cream
1 large onion, cut small
grated parmesan cheese
nutmeg, salt, pepper
crushed garlic
oil for frying
Preheat the oven to 200°C/400°F/Gas Mark 6.

Fry the onion in oil until it is transparent. Then add the defrosted (thawed) spinach and heat through. Stir in the garlic and season with salt, pepper and nutmeg. Pour the mixture into an ovenproof dish. Blend the eggs with the cream and pour the mixture over the spinach. Wait until it has soaked in (you can help a little with a fork). Then sprinkle over the parmesan cheese and place the dish in the heated oven. Bake for about 20 minutes or until the top has turned a little brown and the eggs are set.

The soup kitchen

Vegetable soup

For four people you need:
2 carrots
2 leeks
1 small can of tomatoes
1 large onion
1 red and 1 green pepper
1 cup of frozen green beans
1 stock cube
savory, rosemary, thyme, basil,
    marjoram (or use 1×5ml
    spoon dried mixed herbs)
salt, pepper, chopped parsley
grated parmesan cheese

Chop the onion and cook in a little oil until it is transparent. Cut all the vegetables, apart from the tomatoes and beans, quite small and add to the pan with the herbs, salt and pepper. Cook everything until soft then add the tomatoes. Bring to the boil. Pour in 1 litre of water and add the stock cubes. Cook for about 15 minutes. Season to taste and sprinkle with chopped parsley. Sprinkle with parmesan cheese as desired.

Exotic lentil soup

For four people you need:
1 large onion, chopped
1 leek
1 pepper
about 15 olives
1 large carrot
3 tomatoes
4 potatoes
1 can of lentils
4 frankfurter sausages
2×15ml spoons vinegar
salt, pepper, caraway, thyme
    and basil

Cook the onion in a large covered saucepan until it is transparent. Peel the potatoes, cut them into small pieces and add to the onion with the caraway. Cook until the mixture is soft. Pour in some water and leave the mixture to cook gently for 20 minutes. Now add all the other vegetables which you've cut up small, except for the lentils. Cook for 10 more minutes. Season well with the flavourings.

Now add the lentils and the sausages, cut small. Heat the soup through, stir in the vinegar and serve.

Cabbage hotpot

For four people you need:
1 lb white cabbage
2 litres of stock
1kg potatoes
500g smoked belly of pork
salt, coriander, marjoram

Cut the cabbage into strips. Cook it in the stock for about half an hour. Peel the potatoes and cut into small pieces. Add them to the cabbage and season with salt, coriander and marjoram. Now place the pork in the pan and cook the lot for another half an hour.

Soup tips

If you think there isn't enough liquid in the pot add some more water.

You could use other vegetables, too, left-over cabbage or cauliflower, for example. Or try peas.

Don't use too much of the various flavourings. You'll soon learn how much to use.

Don't overcook the vegetables. They should retain their shape.

We all love pasta

Spaghetti Bolognese

For four people you need:
500g minced (ground) beef
500g spaghetti
1 large onion
1 clove of garlic
1 large can of tomatoes
about 125g of tomato paste
thyme, basil, rosemary, oregano
2 carrots
½ pot single (light) cream
salt, pepper

Fry the beef until it is nicely browned. Then add the thyme, basil, rosemary and the finely copped onion and fry for a few minutes more. Pour in the tomatoes and stir in the tomato paste, crushed garlic and a little water. Grate the carrots over the mixture, cover and cook gently for 1 hour. Stir in the cream and season with salt, pepper and oregano.

Cook the spaghetti in plenty of boiling water with salt and 3×15ml spoons of oil for 10 minutes or until soft.

Green pasta with cream

For four people you need:
500g green pasta
200g streaky bacon
1 large onion
1 clove of garlic
basil, salt, pepper
parmesan cheese,
¼ litre single cream
2 eggs

Cut the bacon very small and fry it until crisp. Then fry the chopped onion, crushed garlic and basil in the bacon fat. Pour in the cream when the onion is soft. Cook everything for a few moments.

Cook the pasta in plenty of salted water. Drain it and mix it with the beaten eggs. Then pour over bacon and cream sauce and mix well. Season with salt and pepper and sprinkle with parmesan.

Home-made pizza

For four people you need:
25g fresh yeast or 1 packet dried
500g flour
2 eggs
wine vinegar
oil or olive oil
oregano, salt
grated cheese (mozzarella is best, but it isn't cheap)
4 tomatoes or onions
And for the topping choose from: anchovies, artichoke hearts, black olives, mushrooms, ham, salami, chillies, anything you can think of and that's available or what the individual eaters choose.

Mix the yeast with a little warm water and 1×5ml of sugar and leave to prove in a warm place. Sift the flour into a large bowl, make a hole in the middle and pour in the yeast mixture. Add two beaten eggs, 1×5ml spoon of vinegar, 3×15ml spoons oil and a cup of lukewarm water and season with 1×5ml spoon of oregano and a little salt. Mix everything well. Then gradually blend in the flour. Knead the dough until it is quite elastic.

Take the dough from the bowl and place it in one hand. With the other hand beat it until it has no small bubbles. Place it in a warm place for proving. Spread the dough on a greased baking sheet and flatten it well. It should be quite thin – you don't want to eat bread but pizza.

Now add the topping. Most important: sprinkle plenty of oregano and cheese over the base. Then top it with what ever you fancy. When the topping is finished, sprinkle it with more cheese and oregano, trickle over some oil and place in the oven. The oven should be preheated to about 250°C/475°F/Gas Mark 8. Bake for about 15 to 20 minutes. Topping and base should be cooked through but not too dry.

Why not try meat?

Super meatballs

For four people you need:
500g minced (ground) beef
2 large onions
4 cloves of garlic
2 eggs, oil, pepper, bread-
    crumbs, nutmeg, salt, oregano
Chop the onions and cook them with the crushed garlic in oil or margarine until softened. Season the mince with salt, pepper, nutmeg and oregano. Add the onions and garlic to the meat, stir in the beaten eggs and 2×15ml spoons of dried breadcrumbs. Mix everything together well. Then shape the mixture into meatballs, roll in some flour and fry in oil until cooked.

Lamb chops

For four people you need:
8 small lamb chops

The night before season the chops with a mixture of:
3×15ml spoons oil, salt, pepper, thyme, basil, rosemary, marjoram and garlic. Cover and keep them in the refrigerator.
The next day fry the chops in oil for 3 minutes on each side. Serve them with green beans and potatoes.

Special goulash

For four people you need:
750g braising steak, cut into
    cubes
about 16 small onions (pickling
    onions)
250g mushrooms
¼ litre red wine
1 cup single (light) cream
salt, pepper, pinch of tarragon
1 bayleaf, 3 sprigs of parsley
Fry the meat in a little oil until nicely browned. Pour in the wine. Transfer the meat to an ovenproof dish with a lid. Stir in the flavourings. Add a little water and place in the preheated oven. Cook for about 1½ hours. Check occasionally whether there's still enough liquid, otherwise add a little more water. Fry the onions in fat and add these and the mushrooms to the meat. Cook for another ½ hour. Test if the meat is tender. If it is, take it out of the oven, remove the bayleaf and parsley sprigs, stir in the cream, heat through on top of the stove and serve.

Sweet dishes

Apple snow

For four people you need:
1 can or jar of apple sauce
2 eggs
a little cinnamon and sugar
Separate the eggs so you have two egg yolks and two egg whites. You won't need the egg yolks. Beat the egg whites until they are stiff. Carefully stir it into the apple sauce. Sprinkle with cinnamon and sugar.

Banana cheese

For four people you need:
500g curd cheese
4 bananas
2 egg yolks
sugar, lemon juice
Whisk the egg yolks with the sugar until foamy. Then stir them into the cheese. Slice the bananas and stir them into the mixture. Add a little lemon juice according to taste.

Fruit salad

For four people you need:
2 oranges
2 bananas
2 apples
a bunch of seedless grapes
a few nuts (walnuts, almonds, hazlenuts)
a little sugar, raisins
Wash the fruit, peel and cut into small pieces. Chop the nuts. Mix everything together in a bowl and leave for half an hour. Tastes super.

Making and Doing

Mobiles
Model-making
Pottery
Printing
Collage
Sewing

Crochet
Knitting
Embroidery
Dolls
Masks
Theatre

Making mobiles

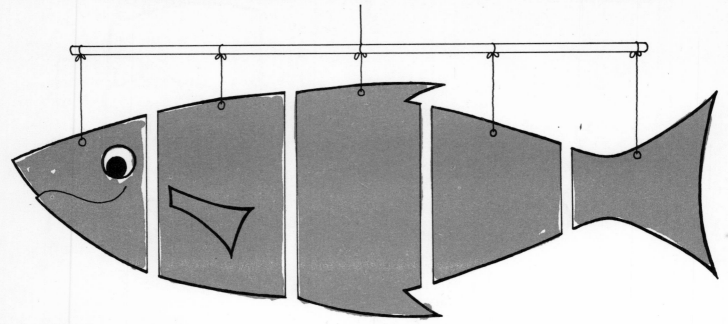

Do you know of anything that moves continuously even if you don't touch it? Yes, it's called a mobile.

'Mobile' means movable, free to move or easily moved. It is also something that moves or causes motion. What we are talking about here is a contraption suspended from threads or thin wire that moves in the slightest current of air in a closed room. So if you want to have something in your room that is 'alive' but doesn't need any care or attention, or if you need new ideas for birthdays or Christmas presents, or if you just want to bring somebody some fun — then why don't you make a mobile? This is how it's done. . . .

You need: straws or thin wooden sticks, thread or florist's wire, a pair of scissors, paper or cardboard and glue.

The dancing fish

A mobile has to be exactly balanced. To learn how to get the balance right, let's do a little preliminary exercise and make a dancing fish. From cardboard cut out a fish shape and divide it into five parts, from head to tail. Colour it brightly and using a needle make a hole where you

suppose the middle or centre of gravity lies. Tie a length of thread to the hole. If the piece hangs straight you found it first go. Congratulations. If it doesn't hang straight — remove the thread, make a new hole and keep trying until it is straight.

Repeat the process with the other pieces (you can cover any surplus holes with paint). Now tie a

thread to a piece of wood the length of your fish and find the correct balance by moving the thread sideways until the stick is exactly horizontal. Make a loop at the top of the thread of each of the five fish pieces and slip them over the stick in the correct sequence. Adjust the loops until all the parts are hanging correctly. Now fasten the threads securely — and you've finished.

Look out, snake!

Our next venture is to make a spiral mobile. On a piece of thin cardboard draw a snake in the shape of a spiral with a dangerous tongue and cut it out. Take a pin with a thick head and glue it

underneath the centre of the snake's tail. Set the point of the needle onto a cork and position the snake over a hot surface like a radiator. The rising warm air will make the snake twist around the cork.

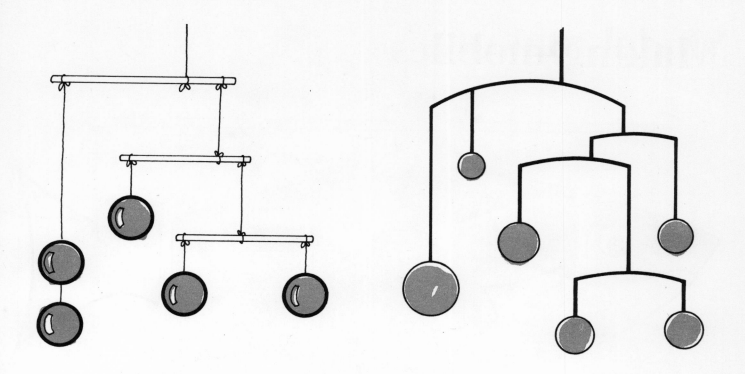

Getting the balance

We have mentioned that balance is all important when making a mobile. Whether you hang three baubles, cardboard shapes or shells on one side, and only one on the other side, the balance depends on how the things are fixed. The horizontal supports needn't be absolutely straight, like wooden sticks or straws. You can also bend some wire into curved shapes.

Try anything that you can think of. Have two baubles on one side, four on the other. And now move the baubles by pushing the threads supporting them from side to side until the correct balance is achieved. It all depends on the length of the 'arms'. We illustrate two possibilities here, but there are many more.

Cat and mouse

Using the balancing trick you can create all sorts of amusing mobiles of your own. Like the cat and mouse mobile in the picture, where the cat will forever chase the two mice. Use a cat shape for one side and two little mice for the other. Hang the mice on a short stick and then the thread of that stick to a longer stick. On the other end of the long stick hang the cat and adjust the balance. In this case the cat will never catch the mice!

Model-making

All toy cars, dolls and playthings could also be called models. If a train is built to a smaller scale it is called a model train. Almost all things of the 'normal' world have a corresponding model. The reason might be that children can learn about the world of the grown-ups through play.

Part of the fun with models is collecting them or swapping them among your friends. You can buy them (not so much fun and rather expensive), or you make them yourself. Try to make a model

aeroplane – you'll see it's not that easy, you have to think it out carefully.

But once your work is complete you'll be proud and satisfied. You might think that one of the wings could have been better or that a particular glue wasn't really suitable; but you'll know how to improve on your construction next time.

You must learn for yourself. That's why you'll find simple building instructions for various models on the following pages. Once you have mastered these you

may want to go on and tackle something a little more complicated. You might visit a model shop, for example, and buy a building plan from which you might attempt the construction of a windmill, a paddle steamer or a biplane, from the planning stage through to the last detail.

It is always advisable to get advice from an adult when using sharp saws or tools. Ask an adult, perhaps your dad or older brother, or even your woodwork teacher, how to hold and use tools properly.

The coastguard boat

This can be built from cardboard. It isn't too difficult and is a good preliminary exercise for further tasks.

Once your coastguard boat is finished you mustn't launch it right away. It needs a coat of paint first.

You can choose the colours yourself, as well as the accessories like lifeboats, the anchor and chains, or the crew.

Materials
shoe box
cardboard box 15×4×9cm
cardboard box 12.5×2.5×5cm
cardboard box 12.5×2.5×2.5cm
thin card 55×27.5cm
cardboard roll
pencil, three matchsticks
glue

Tools
sharp knife
ruler
pencil
pair of scissors

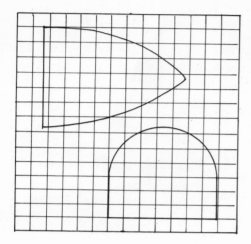

Cut out these pieces from cardboard plus two rectangles, one measuring 55×12.5cm; the other 27.5×11.5cm

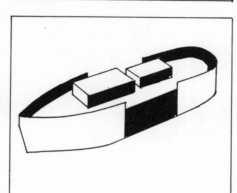

Turn over the shoe box and glue both parts together as illustrated.

Fold the larger rectangle in the middle and stick to the front, and the other to the back. Let one side set first before fixing the other.

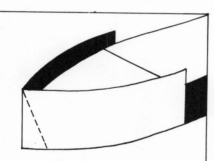

Brush some glue between the edge and the line indicated, press the sides together and cut off the surplus.

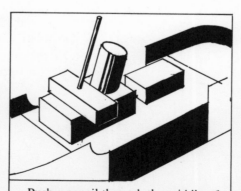

Stick the two bigger boxes in place as shown.

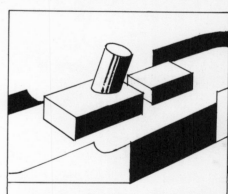

Cut off 6.5cm from the cardboard roll at a slant; glue it to the first box.

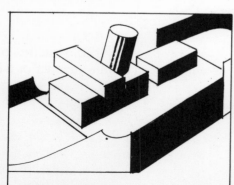

Stick the third box sideways across the centre of the first box in front of the funnel.

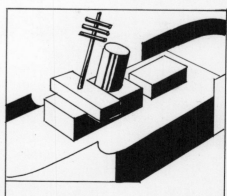

Push a pencil through the middle of the upper box, bend backwards lightly and fasten with glue.

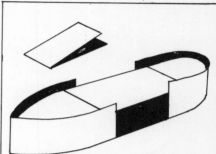

Glue three matchsticks to the mast having cut off the burnt ends first.

99

The old Chinese junk

Your coastguard boat is standing on your shelf (isn't it?). Now if you are ready for bigger things, let's build a Chinese junk.

This time your boat should really float. But that involves working more carefully than before.

Once your junk is finished try it out in the bathtub. Blow against the sail and see whether it works.

Materials

thick cardboard 40×48cm
thick, flexible card 20×57.5cm
stiff paper 45×45cm

case from a ballpoint pen
wooden stick 55cm
thin wooden stick 15cm
plywood 7.5×5cm
muslin 15×5cm
4 sticks from an ice lolly (flat)
piece of wood 9×1.25×1.25cm
strong glue
oil paints, clear varnish
sand or gravel, about 1.5kgs

Tools

ruler, pencil, sharp knife, drill, 0.5cm, round file.

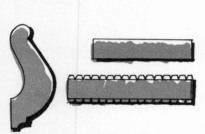

From thick cardboard cut two pieces for the hull, from thin card, rectangles 45×8cm and 57.5×11.25cm. Cut notches 1.25cm deep into the larger rectangle.

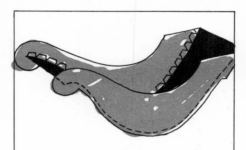

Fold over the notched edges and stick them to the lower edges of the hull pieces. Paint all the parts six times with oil paint.

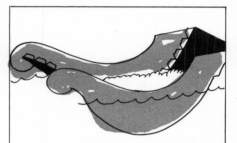

Fill the hull with the sand and test whether it floats. There must be enough sand in the hull so that the lowest point lies 3cm above the water level.

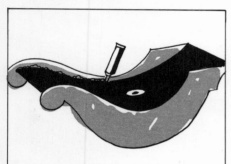

Make a hole in the middle of the other rectangle. Stick it to the boat at the front and back. Brush glue along the sides. Paint the deck three times.

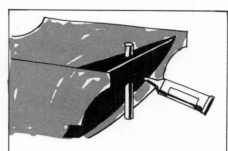

Drill a hole through the centre of the deck at the stern 2.5cm from the edge. Saw off 9.75cm from the ball point case and stick it in the hole so that it protrudes 2.5cm from the top.

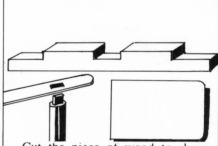

Cut the piece of wood to shape. Flatten the end of the thin stick. Make a slit into the ice lolly stick so that the top fits into it. File the corners of the plywood round.

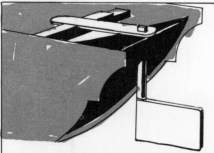

Fix the rudder with glue and cover it with muslin. Then paint it three times. Insert the stick in the ball point case, stick on the ice lolly stick. Glue the piece of wood across the quarterdeck.

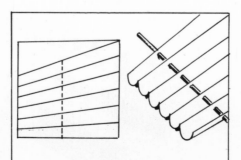

Cut out the sail. Make holes 1.25cm from the lines. Fold the sail at the lines; push through the mast, fold the sail and glue it.

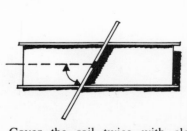

Cover the sail twice with clear varnish. Push the mast through the deck into the sand. Glue it in place at an angle of 45° to the deck. Adjust the balance with the sail and rudder.

The ship in a bottle

Now we come to a clever piece of work: the ship in the bottle.

Don't worry, that too can be managed and become a show-piece of your collection. Once you've mastered the construction of a bottle ship with this simple example you'll probably want to make more. You could try and get hold of some plans of old sailing ships; have a look in some books borrowed from the library.

Materials

clear glass bottle 12.5cm long, 6.5cm diameter ·
balsa wood 10×7.5×1.3cm
strong white paper 15×7.5cm
flat wooden sticks 25×0.5cm
3 wooden toothpicks
nails of equal thickness
strong glue, paints

Tools

sharp knife, steel ruler
medium and fine sandpaper
wire 40cm
pliers, scissors, pencil

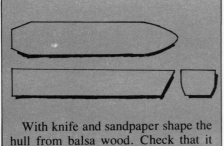

With knife and sandpaper shape the hull from balsa wood. Check that it will pass through the bottle neck.

Using a nail, punch holes in the deck at a distance of 2cm, and one in the bow. Paint the hull.

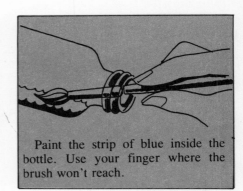

Paint the strip of blue inside the bottle. Use your finger where the brush won't reach.

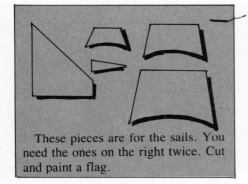

These pieces are for the sails. You need the ones on the right twice. Cut and paint a flag.

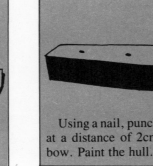

Make three masts and the bowsprit from toothpicks. (Make them 1.5cm shorter than the cross-section of the bottle.

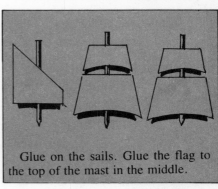

Glue on the sails. Glue the flag to the top of the mast in the middle.

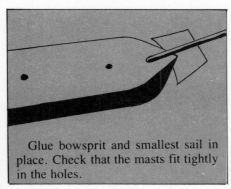

Glue bowsprit and smallest sail in place. Check that the masts fit tightly in the holes.

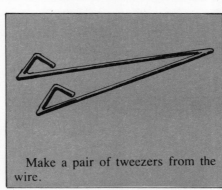

Make a pair of tweezers from the wire.

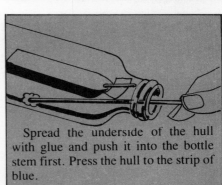

Spread the underside of the hull with glue and push it into the bottle stem first. Press the hull to the strip of blue.

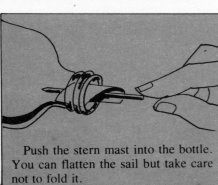

Push the stern mast into the bottle. You can flatten the sail but take care not to fold it.

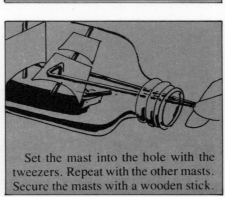

Set the mast into the hole with the tweezers. Repeat with the other masts. Secure the masts with a wooden stick.

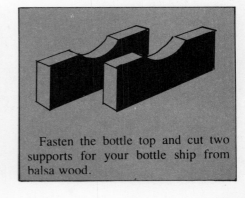

Fasten the bottle top and cut two supports for your bottle ship from balsa wood.

The pirate ship

When overseas trading began in the Middle Ages between Europe and her colonies in America and Asia it was also the beginning of piracy. Most pirates were resistance fighters against foreign rule in their own country and by raiding rich trading vessels procured money and weapons for the uprisings.

There were a lot of pirate ships sailing the oceans at that time. The trading fleets of all countries were never safe against them. The pirates possessed fast, agile ships and daring crews which consisted mainly of freed convicts, oppressed and impoverished people. The captains of these ships were often dispossessed noblemen or officers of warships who had quit service under their kings. They were well trained in navigation and warfare and soon taught the skippers of trading ships to fear them.

One of the most famous pirates was the Black Corsair who, with his men, fought for the independence of the Mediterranean island of Corsica. It was whispered behind closed doors at the time that the Black Corsair was a French count who was banished from his homeland. Another version said that he became a pirate because of an unhappy love affair.

His ship 'Liberty', which means freedom, is the model we are going to build here. So get a knife, glue and paintbrush ready and begin.

Materials

balsa wood 11×2.5×2.5cm
balsa wood 6×6×2.5cm
thick white paper 18×15cm
card
box lid 20×15×2.5cm
12 toothpicks
black thread, polystyrene
model enamel paints
glue, household candle
thin tube, small round nail

Tools

pencil, paper knife
ruler, paintbrush
fine saw
sharp scissors
file, tweezers
sandpaper

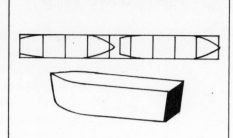

Draw the above outlines onto the block of wood. Cut out the hull with a saw and sandpaper it smooth.

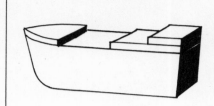

Glue the pieces of balsa wood to the deck as above. Smooth down with sandpaper and paint the entire hull.

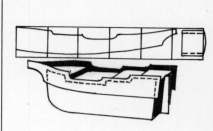

Cut card to above shape. Stick on the rudder. Glue on the sides so they stick out.

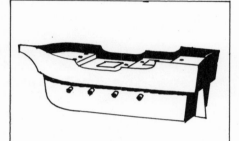

Stick on the rear. Make guns, portholes and capstan from cardboard and toothpicks and glue in place.

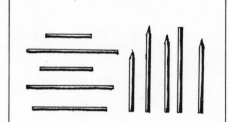

Cut out masts and spars from toothpicks (length above). Careful: some have points, others haven't.

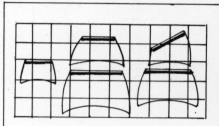

Cut sails from thick paper. Roll them so they arch. Stick them to the respective spars.

Glue the spars to the masts, stick the masts into the holes on the deck. Arrange the sails as illustrated.

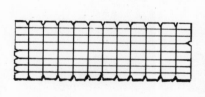

Draw this pattern exactly onto cardboard (7.5×2.5cm). Cut in the notches. Rub the cardboard with the candle.

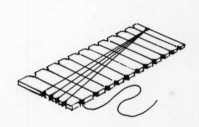

Stretch the thread from the upper notch to the first lower notch, then back, then to the second, etc. Then stretch it across the horizontal notches.

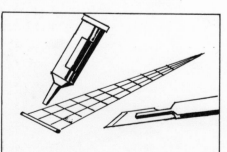

Varnish the threads. Cut 6 sticks, 1cm long. Glue to the rigging and cut off from the card.

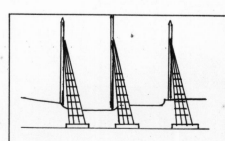

Prepare 2 more pieces of rigging with card front and 3 with card back. Glue to the mast and hull.

Brush the top of the box lid with glue for waves. Stick on the ship. Cut wave crests from polystyrene.

The glider

Now we depart from water and waves and suggest building an aeroplane, a glider that can really fly.

That, too, isn't as difficult as it might appear. But you'll need a little intuition to get the balance right. And how is the finished plane started? By holding the fuselage between thumb and forefinger and throwing the glider into the air.

Tools

sharp knife, steel ruler
fine saw, paintbrush
medium and fine sandpaper

Materials

pieces of soft balsa wood
   53×8×0.5cm
battens of hard balsa wood
   53×1×0.5cm
   53×2×0.25cm
   23×7×0.125cm
quick-drying glue
varnish and thinner
sticky tape and 3 pins
hardwood 2×3×15cm
lead weight 2.5×1×0.25cm

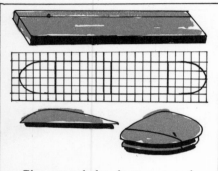

Glue two balsa battens together, sandpaper to shape shown and cut in four pieces. Sand the corners round and flat.

Grind down the ends of the larger piece. Lay one piece flat, add the other at an angle by supporting it with a block of wood (2cm).

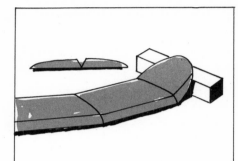

Glue the wingtips to the centre piece (use 3cm hardwood for support). Leave both sides to set.

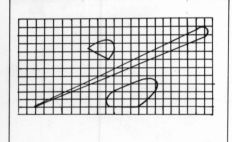

Cut the fuselage from 0.25cm balsa wood and the tail pieces from 0.125cm.

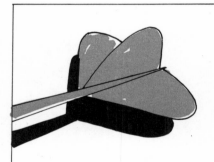

Glue the tailplane to the bottom end of the fuselage, exactly in the centre. Glue the rudder to the top on one side of the fuselage.

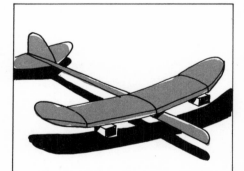

Glue the wings 11.25cm from the front tip. Place 2cm pieces of balsa wood underneath to check the balance.

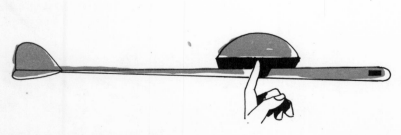

Glue a 0.125cm in triangle of balsa wood underneath the wing (left for left-handed, right for right-handed people). Smooth all edges round with sandpaper.

Brush the wood with thinned varnish and sand smooth. Fasten the weight to the nose and balance the plane on your forefinger.

Test: push the plane downwards into the air. If it rises up, add more weight to the front. If it dives down, file the nose down a little.

The sky-dasher

After the rather difficult models on the previous pages we come to something easy for a change. A plane that you can launch into the air with a catapult. So get going and make your sky-dasher — but never aim it at people or animals.

Materials

balsa wood 7.5×40×0.25cm
glue, oil or cellulose paints
empty toothpaste or glue tube
stick 15×0.5cm, pin
elastic band, tracing paper

Tools

sharp knife, pencil, scissors
steel ruler, sandpaper

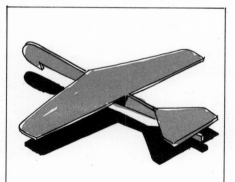

Draw the above pattern on tracing paper.

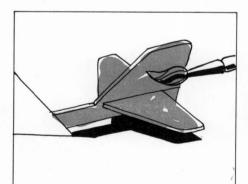

Pin the paper to the balsa wood and pierce the outlines with a pin.

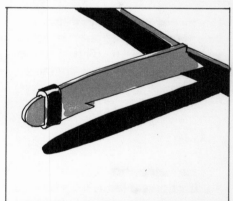

Cut out the pieces with a knife and steel ruler. Smooth down the rounded corners with sandpaper.

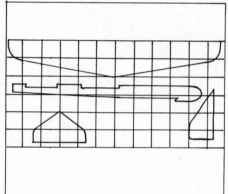

Glue on wings and tailplane. Take care that they are perfectly centred and lined up.

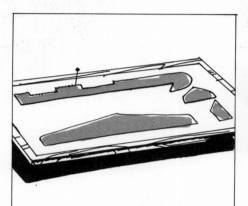

Glue the tailplane to the tailpiece. Paint three times, sanding down between coats.

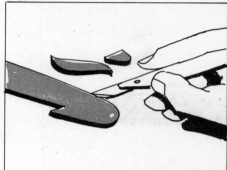

Cut off a piece from the empty tube and wind it over the nose of the plane.

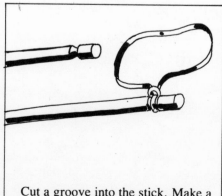

Cut a groove into the stick. Make a knot in the elastic band and loop it over the groove.

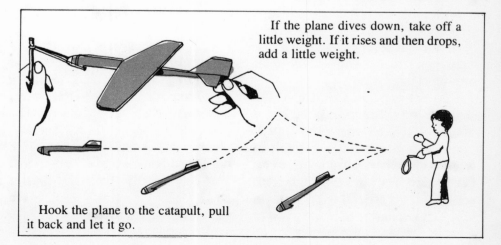

Hook the plane to the catapult, pull it back and let it go.

If the plane dives down, take off a little weight. If it rises and then drops, add a little weight.

Clay modelling

There is a material that will retain any shape that you give it. It's so elastic and flexible that you can mould it into any shape that you can think of. The material is clay and with it your imagination can become reality.

Clay

Our ancestors discovered the value of clay a long, long time ago. It is from archaeological finds of pottery and other artefacts that we learn about ancient cultures.

Some of the first walls were constructed from clay. They could be built quite high and with a smooth surface. And a clay wall provided insulation.

Clay is a very useful material for shaping and modelling. But it is not often possible to work with clay at home. Not because it's difficult to work with but because it has to be fired (hardened) at very high temperatures in a special oven called a kiln – much hotter than the oven at home.

You may have the opportunity to try pottery, perhaps at school or with a local potter, where there is a kiln available to fire the pots.

Otherwise, there are other materials with which you can obtain similar results. These don't need any firing at all, or they can be fired in your oven at home.

Plastic clay for your oven

This type of clay can be fired in your oven at 175°C/350°F/Gas Mark 4. It has the added advantage that it can be bought in many different colours. You only need to varnish it after firing.

Plaster of Paris

Plaster of Paris is another material very suitable for modelling. But take care to mix it by adding the powder to the water, not the other way round. The higher the proportion of water to plaster the thinner the paste will be. One advantage of plaster is that you can actually pour the plaster paste into moulds. Later the mixture will harden and can be sculpted with a knife.

Clays that harden in the air

There are some artificial materials available that resemble natural clay quite closely. One advantage is that they don't need firing as they harden in the air. When the hardened material is submerged in water for a few days it becomes flexible again and can be reformed. Ask about these products at your local craft shop.

Paper pulp as a wood substitute

Water mixed with powdered wood pulp makes a modelling material. It hardens in the air and takes on the properties of wood. You can carve it just like wood. Ask in craft shops for instant papiermâché.

Filler pastes

Filler pastes that are used to fill cracks on walls are even better than Plaster of Paris. These products, Polyfilla for example, have a longer setting time than plaster. You therefore have more time to work the material before it hardens. That's a great advantage for the beginner.

Basket pottery

One form of pottery is basket pottery. Take a ball of clay or your chosen material and a small basket, a bread basket for instance. Press a layer of clay onto the basket bottom and spread it evenly over the entire inside of the basket. Press it down as evenly as possible. When all is covered smooth the clay down with your fingers or a damp sponge. As the clay dries in the air you have a 'double' effect

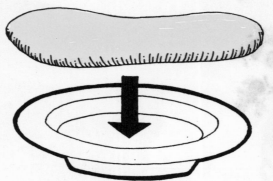

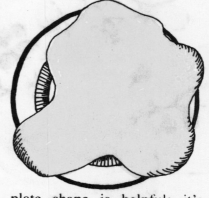

for your dish: inside clay, outside basket.

But you could also use the basket as a mould to give you the basket pattern. After you have pressed the clay inside the basket remove the clay layer carefully and repair any damaged or thin areas.

Above, we've done the same with a china plate. It's obvious that the resulting clay print will be smaller than the original plate. But

the plate shape is helpful; it's rather difficult to make an evenly round plate shape without a potter's wheel.

The clay ball

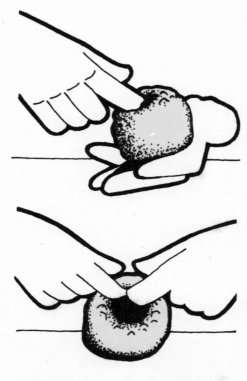

The simplest way to shape a hollow thing from clay is to use a ball of clay. Roll a ball from the clay material, turn it in your hands until it is really nice and round. Now with your finger carefully make a hole in the ball. With your fingers form the walls from the inside outwards. The ball will grow, the walls will become thinner and higher. If you carefully press the ball together with both hands you'll have a vase shape. If you gently press it together at the opening it becomes fat-bellied.

If you now carefully press the opening edge together with your fingertips and round it off, you'll have a rim. You could shape another lip at its edge or leave it as it is. In the same manner you could form a spout into the edge which will make pouring easier later.

Coil pots

You can produce many different shapes using this technique. At first make several drawings of your planned project. Then decide which drawing to use and form the base from a lump of clay. The edge must be clean and smooth. To begin with it is probably easier to cut out the bottom as you would cut a biscuit out of dough.

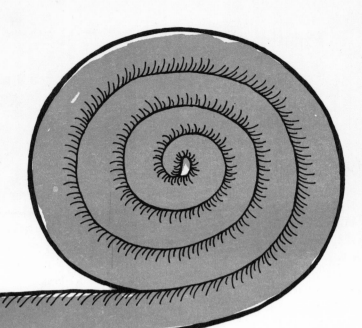

Then make a sausage shape — make sure it's smooth and free of air bubbles — and flatten it with your fist or the flat of your hand. Coil the flattened sausage over the base of your pot pressing it firmly all round the edge. When you have completed the circle, break off. Continue placing band upon band until your pot is finished. Fill the gaps carefully with clay.

You can use this technique to produce large or square pots and vases.

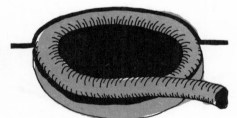

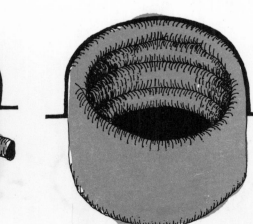

Finishing off

Once your shape has hardened or been fired it must be finished off. You could paint it, for example. Ask at a craft or hobby shop which paint is most suitable for your material. Buy the right brushes at the same time. And now — you can let loose your imagination.

Flower shapes are suitable for almost any vessel. You can paint from nature or invent your own designs. You could paint vertical stripes of different colours, or you could try horizontal stripes.

On egg cups, for example, you might paint a chicken family or the names of your parents, brothers and sisters. You could make a feeding bowl for your cat and paint it with lots of mice, although it probably eats enough already. Or you could look up in your story-books and copy classical shapes.

Plaster prints

You can make the most fascinating things from plaster — because plaster or Polyfilla can be used in a liquid state.

To begin with you must prepare the mixture properly. You don't need many implements, just common sense. You must start by pouring the correct amount of water into a vessel (using a plastic bowl makes cleaning up afterwards easier as you can bend the sides to break out any dried plaster).

Now add the plaster and stir continuously with your free hand using a wooden stick or similar.

Scratch a picture into sand and pour in the runny plaster mixture. Wait until the plaster sets, take it off the sand and brush it off. You now have a true print of your picture.

Or if you find some animal tracks in the sand, put in a little plaster and you'll have excellent prints for your track collection.

Press your bare foot into the sand and surround the area with a

wall of sand. You can now make your own plaster foot print. You could do the same with your hands, of course. If you want to puzzle your friends make a print with each of your feet side by side but cross-wise, and make a cast of your two feet pointing in different directions.

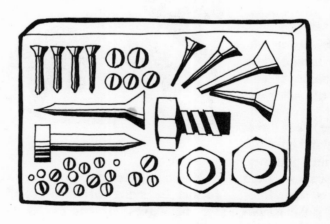

The powder will thicken into a grey mass so add it very gradually and check on the consistency.

Now you can have some fun, particularly if you have a supply of sand nearby.

Coin and nail reliefs

You can do a lot more with plaster. Nothing is easier than making coin prints. Fasten a strip of cardboard around the edge of your coin before covering it with plaster. If you incorporate a little ring you can wear your plaster coin around your neck on a chain.

You can make nice moulds for relief pictures from Plasticine. Simply press objects like coins or

nails into the Plasticine. Don't forget to surround the Plasticine mould with a rim. Pour in the plaster mixture and leave to set. Afterwards carefully pull off the Plasticine. Any remains of Plasticine can be removed with a brush.

Fun with prints

You can print almost anything and there is no limit to the materials you can use. The only thing you must have is paper and paint, but even here there are various possibilities: water colours, oil paints, or special printing inks.

You could begin by using old rags, net curtains or threads and covering them with paint. If you press them on a piece of paper you will get a print.

Depending on the way you arrange your design, and in what order, you can print patterns, pictures, entire landscapes. Take the leaf of a maple or oak tree, cover it with paint and press it onto paper; the result is probably much more impressive than painstakingly drawing it (see below).

You could develop your picture further by using different colours for the leaves, or you could stay with one colour and alter the picture by arranging the leaves in a certain pattern. You could, per-

haps, create a whole tree by using prints of many leaves.

You can also print with a stamp you've made yourself. Cut out the design, a horse for example, from thick cardboard and glue it to an old stamp or something similar. Now press the stamp first onto an ink pad and then onto your paper.

Cover a tennis ball with paint and squeeze it in various ways onto your paper. You won't believe what super effects you can create that way.

You probably know about making symmetrical butterflies or other fantastic images. Fold a piece of paper in the middle and sprinkle paint or ink on one side. Fold it over and open it up again: you can now try your luck at interpreting the various shapes.

Use the same paint, but different printing-blocks.

The same blocks, but different colours (you must cut several blocks with the same shape, otherwise the old colour might come through with the new colour).

Different shapes and colours — you should make a pattern for the desired picture beforehand. Then print the same shape and colour before changing colour and shape.

To make an exact, repeating pattern you should make some templates from wood or cardboard first, and then start printing.

Potato prints

For most people printing with potatoes is the beginning of their printing hobby. Printing with potatoes is simple and cheap (you will almost always find a few potatoes at home).

The potatoes are first washed and cut in half. The cut edge is used for printing. You can cut many different printing-blocks from potatoes, as in the sample above: circles, rectangles, stripes . . . Or you can hollow out the potato, cut bizarre shapes — there are no restrictions!

You can use any water-soluble paint for printing, poster paints, tempera and water colours.

The paint can be brushed onto the potato — or the potato can be dipped into the paint. But it is best if the paint is spread onto a suitable surface (a piece of glass or a plate) beforehand, otherwise the potato will take up too much paint and the print will be smudged.

And, again, there are many possibilities for the printing itself:

You can make a pattern using the same printing-block again and again, spread evenly with paint before each print.

Make a pattern with the same printing-block using various shades of the same colour, using the block several times before applying the new paint.

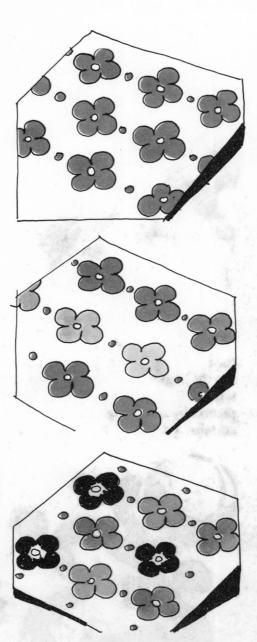

Printing with stencils

If you want to print repeating patterns which will fit edge to edge exactly, or curved lines and difficult shapes, perhaps on to a wall or sheet, it is best to cut out a stencil. That is the name for a pattern where the space to be printed is cut out and at the same time the space that's not to be printed is covered.

You can cut a stencil from waxed paper by first drawing your design and then carefully cutting it out. Use thick paints, preferably, so they don't run under the stencil paper and smudge your picture. And you must cut a new stencil for each new colour!

The lino cut

The lino cut is not so different from printing with potatoes or stencils and not very much more difficult. The parts not to be coloured are cut out, the coloured parts remain.

What do you need?

Pieces of linoleum and various cutting blades which can be pushed into a special handle. We have illustrated below the most important kinds of blades; in addition, we explain how you should cut: the edges must not be too small or narrow as they quickly break — therefore always cut cone-shaped profiles.

On the big picture above you see all the things that you need for lino cutting: the cutting blades and holder, paint, sponge to wipe the lino, etc. Below right you see which blade you need for which type of cut. But you better try for yourself!

And a few general tips: Don't use shiny paper for printing as it will not take the paint properly. It is best to use card or fine paper. You can buy the printing ink and lino cutting tools in craft shops.

You also need a tool with which you can press the paper hard onto the lino cut. You can use an old spoon, or a small pastry roller, but a rubber roller is even better.

You must try to work very cleanly as even the smallest smudge on the paper will spoil the effect. Get hold of a lot of old rags with which you can wipe off any spilled paint straight away.

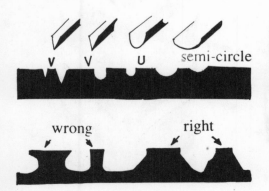

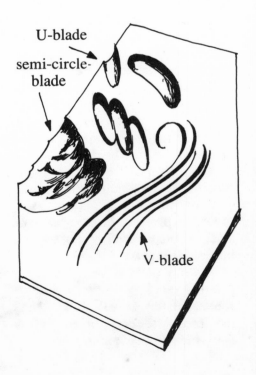

U-blade
semi-circle-blade
V-blade

1

Draw your desired design on a piece of paper and transfer it to the piece of linoleum.

With the various blades cut out the areas that are not to be coloured, always pushing the blade away from you to avoid cutting yourself.

2

Spread the printing ink evenly over a piece of glass.

3

Then roll the roller backwards and forwards on the paint until it is evenly covered. Now roll the paint evenly over the lino cut.

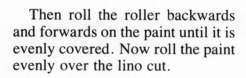

4

Place a piece of paper or card over the printing-block and press it down firmly with a spoon or a press.

Carefully pull the paper off the block. Before making a new print you must apply more ink.

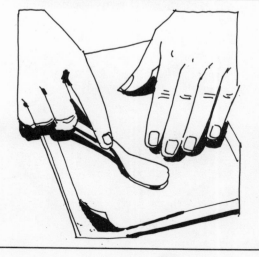

Screen printing

Don't be put off by the technical term for this type of printing: screen printing. Although you need a few more implements than with the other methods we've described you will get some rather professional looking results. And it is a rather professional type of printing, many posters or T-shirts you see in the shops are screen printed.

The screen consists of a wooden frame which is covered with net (gauze or net curtain). If you want

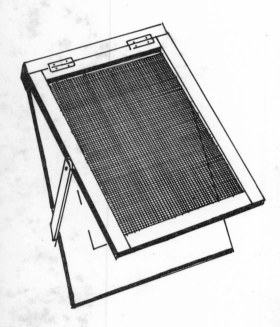

to make your own frame you must ensure that it is bigger than the desired size of your print. Glue four battens together and secure them with nails or pins. The frame must lay level on the surface.

Fasten the netting to the frame with staples. It must be stretched taut over the frame and completely parallel.

Now you need a base to take the paper or material you are printing on, preferably the base should be fastened to the frame by a hinge (as in the drawing) to keep it stable — and you can mark it with lines for positioning. A strut for holding the frame open is quite easy to make, too.

Now you need a spatula, a length of wood with a rubber edge

with which you spread the paint over the netting. It should be 1cm smaller than the frame.

Masking tape along the edges of the screen prevents the paint from running into the frame.

To print your design you must, again, prepare a stencil or

template, but in this case it can be made from newspaper. The template must be the 'negative' picture, that means everything that you wish to appear in print must be cut out of the template — and vice versa. Fasten the outer edges of the template to the frame with sticky tape, loose pieces can be stuck down with a thin film of clear glue.

Now place the paper on the base underneath the screen. If you want

to make several prints take care that you position the paper in the same place each time — using your positioning lines mentioned earlier.

Place your choice of paint from a jar or a tube on the screen. Take the spatula in both hands and draw it over the screen so that the paint is spread evenly and prints on the paper where the template isn't covering it.

The surplus paint can be returned with the spatula. Open up the frame, remove the paper, insert a new sheet and print again.

Making a rainbow

Rainbows are seen whenever sunshine shines through a fine spray of water, such as the spray from a waterfall, or a garden hose, and especially raindrops. The coloured lights of a rainbow are there all the time but we see them all jumbled up and therefore they look white. The drops of water split up the white light into separate colours of the spectrum. This is the correct name for the colours of the rainbow. One way to produce a rainbow is to fill a bowl with water and place it in a sunny position.

Facing a mirror towards the sun, dip it into the water but tilt it at an angle. This will produce a rainbow on the ceiling.

Another way is to put a glass of water on a sunny windowsill or hold it up to the sunlight. Move it about or tilt it slightly and you will see a rainbow on the ceiling or the floor. Put a piece of white paper on the floor to show the rainbow more clearly.

Do you know the colours of the rainbow?

Here is the easy way to remember the order of the colours of the rainbow. This rhyme will always remind you:

Richard	red
of	orange
York	yellow
gained	green
battles	blue
in	indigo
vain	violet

Let's make a collage

If you don't fancy drawing why don't you make a collage. You'll see that you can produce collages with many different materials, each a new variation.

You can find materials everywhere. Don't throw anything away and you'll soon have a collection of things for all kinds of collages. Look for scraps of material at home, sea-shells on the beach, leaves in the woods and gardens,

and flowers, too. Old magazines are useful, so are buttons you can beg from your mother — and if you gained quite a bit of experience in making collages and can produce beautiful things, perhaps someone will give you a packet of sequins — or you could ask for them for your birthday.

The most important techniques of collage are glueing and sewing. Here are a few ideas:

The tree in your room

Collect lots of different leaves. Wash them and place them first between sheets of blotting paper, then between some heavy books for several days. Then draw a very

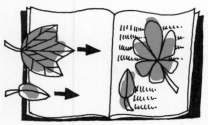

large tree-trunk and branches on several pieces of card. Glue the card together — the tree can be as tall as your room! Stick the pressed leaves to the branches with a little glue. Or you could stick the tree directly to the wall. That looks even nicer, but it will destroy your wallpaper so discuss it with your parents first.

116

Fabric collages

Take a thick piece of fabric — sacking is suitable, or felt. Cut out shapes from scraps of material and sew them to the base fabric.

You can produce anything from a fantasy zoo to ships in a harbour. Or you can decorate table napkins, tablecloths, even curtains with your own designs. But you

should make a plan, a sketch, to help you to decide on the arrangement of colours, fabrics and shapes. This will help you to avoid a disastrous result!

The landscape

Take a piece of card and paint it any colour you like. Then glue on sea-shells in such a way that they look like trees, houses, roads, church spires . . . anything you can think of.

Only use as little glue as possible as dried glue will spoil the picture.

Group picture

Cut out heads of people from magazines. You can arrange them according to groups: film stars, politicians, football players, pop stars. Or you can mix them. Then arrange them to your liking and stick them on strong paper.

Some heads could be upside down. Or put a politician's head with the legs of a football player.

Or top the bodies of film stars with the heads of politicians. You can produce paper collages by printing and colouring, too. Look it up in the chapter about printing. Or you can make a mixed collage:

Sew real buttons to the suit of a man, or make a three-dimensional collage. If, for example, you take as your background the photo of a room you could glue in a table-leg, a matchbox, a tablecloth or an egg cup. It gives quite a crazy impression!

117

Needlework – just for girls?

People really used to think that there were certain things that only girls were supposed to do and certain things that only boys were supposed to do. Don't you believe it! There are men who knit, boys who make dolls as well as girls who play football and repair old furniture. It's the same with sewing, crochet and other 'needlework'. It is not only useful to know how to sew on a button or mend a tear in a shirt. Just think, you could wear a pullover you made all by yourself, or your jeans could be covered with appliqués you sewed on yourself. There is nothing girlish about that! Just try it. Such work requires patience but you need that for fishing, too. Once you can see the first results needlework isn't a chore any more as you will see. . . .

The tools

You won't need a lot as most things are available in your household anyway: sewing and knitting needles, crochet hooks, cotton, wool, pieces of fabric, scissors and pins, but to begin with, a needle threader, perhaps, and a thimble.

Running stitch

With this stitch you can sew pieces of material together. Place the pieces of fabric on top of each other (pattern on pattern, wrong sides facing outwards) and secure

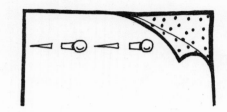

them with pins so they won't slide apart. Take a needle and thread. Pass the needle from underneath to the top and down again, in and out.

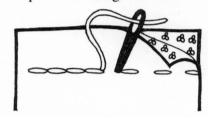

Don't make the stitches too big.

When you have finished the seam you can fill in the spaces between the stitches. This is called backstitch.

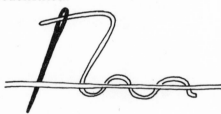

Hemming

With this stitch you fasten hems. Fold over the edge of the material a little bit and then again a little wider. Secure the hem with pins. Then sew it up, catching only a thread on the right side of the fabric and using a longer stitch on the wrong side. With a little practice you will soon be able to sew tidy hems.

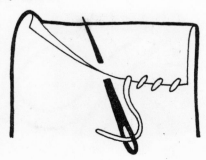

Oversewing

This is a more decorative stitch as it doesn't disappear like the running stitch when you turn the work over. With it you can join edges together. It is better to use thicker thread for this.

Place two pieces of fabric together, wrong side to wrong side this time. Secure them with pins. Insert the needle from back to front. Place the thread over the edge, insert the needle again, and so on.

First project: a scarf

Choose a nice piece of material and cut it to the size required for your scarf. Just hem all four edges – and your scarf is finished.

Second project: a book cover

To make a book cover place the opened book on the piece of fabric and cut it so that there is a fairly small edge at the top and bottom and about 5cm on either side. First

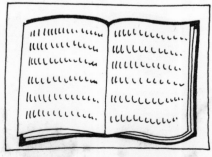

you hem all the edges. Then fasten the side loops with pins and sew

Blanket stitch

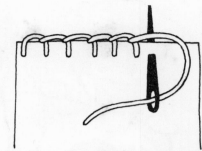

This is another stitch for finishing edges and neatly done it looks very attractive. Pin two pieces of fabric together as for oversewing. This time place the thread around the point of the needle before you insert the needle in the back.

Sewing on buttons

Stitch from bottom to top, first through the fabric, then through a hole in the button. Then back through the other hole and the fabric. Repeat until you think the button is secure. Don't cut off the thread until you have properly fastened it off.

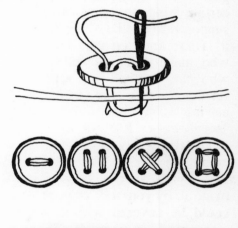

them to top and bottom with oversewing or blanket stitch.

Crochet

To crochet you need yarn or wool and a crochet hook the same thickness as your wool.

Pull the end of the wool from the ball over your hand, between your little finger and ring finger, and out between middle finger and index finger. Hold the thread between your thumb and middle finger.

With the other hand hold the crochet hook like a pencil with the hook pointing towards you.

1

Make a loop at the beginning of the thread and pull through the thread coming from the ball.

2

When you pull the drawn thread into a loop you will secure the starting loop at the same time.

3

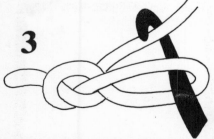

Now hook the thread coming from the other hand through the loop again with the crochet hook. This type of thread formation is called *chain*.

4

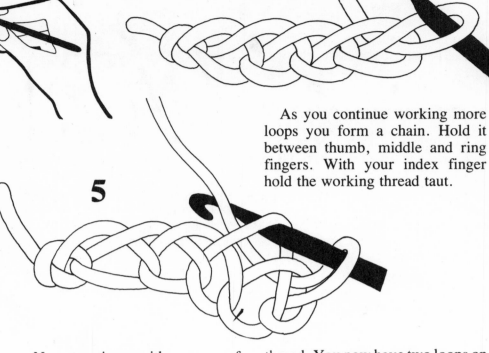

As you continue working more loops you form a chain. Hold it between thumb, middle and ring fingers. With your index finger hold the working thread taut.

5

Now continue with a row of double crochet. For this insert the hook into the third stitch from the end and form a loop with the thread. You now have two loops on your hook. (Gently pull the thread until both loops are of even size. Hook in the working thread.)

6

7

Pull the working thread both loops at once. Continue to crochet this way by hooking loop by loop through both loops on the hook. At the end of the row make a chain stitch so you can set another row on top.

Pot-holders . . .

Take fairly thick cotton yarn and a fat crochet hook. Crochet a square shape for a pot-holder. You can also make patterns by using different colours. For this you have to knot together the old and the new thread.

Knitting

1

Knitting, too, is no big problem once you have mastered the art of crochet. To begin with make a chain with the crochet hook, as you have learned.

2

Now take a knitting needle in your right hand and with it pull a loop through each stitch of the chain and leave it on the needle.

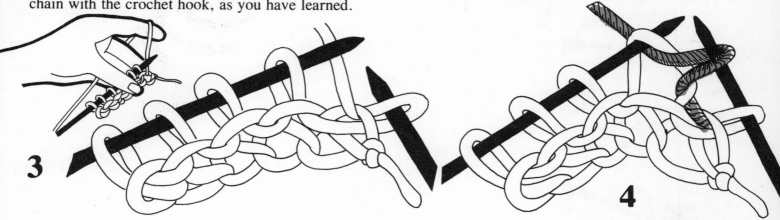

3

When you have picked up all the stitches take the needle in your hand as shown on the picture. Hold the working thread tight with your index finger. Take the second needle in your right hand and with it lift off the first stitch.

4

Now insert the right needle from the front to the back through the following stitch on the left side. Pull the working thread through this stitch leaving the loop on the right needle. Pull the stitch off the left needle. Continue with the next stitch.

Once you have finished knitting you have to cast off. Lift off the first stitch and knit the second as usual. Then pull the first loop over the second stitch. Knit another stitch, pull the first over the second. Repeat until all the stitches have been cast off.

Patchwork blanket

The patchwork blanket consists of a series of crocheted or knitted squares sewn together. Use a different colour for each square and your blanket will be nice and colourful.

5

Knitting ideas

Of course pot-holders can be knitted, too. Or a woolly scarf. Cast on as many stitches as your scarf is going to be wide. Then knit until you have reached the desired length. To make a knitted cushion cover work out the number of stitches needed for the width of the cushion and knit until the piece is twice as long as the cushion. Sew the edges together afterwards.

121

Embroidery for jeans

Embroidery looks very good on jeans. Work out your design and draw it on tracing paper. Place it over the fabric and embroider through the paper and fabric. Afterwards, carefully pull out the paper from underneath the thread. It is best to use special embroidery thread.

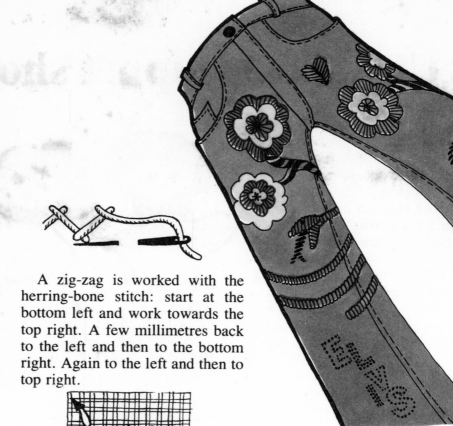

For a rope-like effect, work from left to right, making close diagonal stitches keeping the thread above the needle.

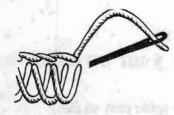

The same basic principle combined with a loop. To make the loops the same length wind them round a pencil.

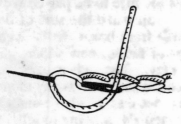

A chain is formed if you bring the needle up, make a loop, insert the needle again at the starting point, make a stitch through the back of the fabric and pull the needle through to catch the loop.

Flowers are made with a daisy stitch, by arranging chain stitches in a star shape and securing each loop with a small stitch.

A zig-zag is worked with the herring-bone stitch: start at the bottom left and work towards the top right. A few millimetres back to the left and then to the bottom right. Again to the left and then to top right.

Cross stitch: for horizonal lines work the left-right stitches first.

Then reverse by stitching right-left (with coarser fabric it is possible to count the threads.

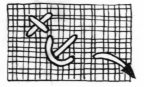

If you want the crosses to slope at an angle you have to complete each cross before you stitch the next.

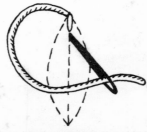

This illustration shows how you have to arrange the stitches to arrive at a leaf shape.

After working a starting stitch at the top, stitch first down one side, then return to the top and stitch the other side.

To make a small knot: Bring out the needle, wind the thread several times around the point of the needle and put the needle in again near the starting point.

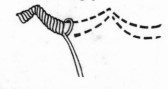

Scallops and corners: the outline of the desired shape is first worked with running stitches, then filled in with satin stitch.

122

Let's have a puppet show

Of course you could always go to the nearest toy shop and buy a nice big plastic doll which can say 'Hello, Mummy!' in a squeaky voice. And you can buy toys and puppets representing your favourite cartoon characters. These are fine in their own way, but there are many other interesting sorts of dolls and puppets. Dolls you can make for yourself and puppets with characters all of their own who can perform in your own puppet theatre.

. . . after your own fashion

It is quite easy to make yourself a doll from bits and pieces you may have around the house. They needn't be wonderfully sculptured dolls, beautifully dressed and almost too nice to be played with.

You can make the sort of doll you like from boxes, balls, wool, scraps of fabric, newspaper, glue and clay. The advantages are obvious, it hardly costs any money and no one else will have one like it. So nobody is going to tell you what your doll is called or what sort of 'character' it has.

Finger puppets

Finger puppets are best made from ping-pong balls. Paint on different faces and stick on hair made from wool. You can make hats, too. Make holes in the balls so they fit nicely over your fingers. And there is your first home made doll. Put on some (preferably white) gloves. Now you can play with several puppets at the same time.

Give them life

You can really bring your dolls to life. You can imagine, from the way you make and dress your dolls, where they might live or what they might do.

In fact, you could write a script for them and have them act it out. We describe how in the chapter about theatre. Puppets, masks and theatre all belong together – so read up on them there.

Any old sock . . .

Old socks are excellent for making a toy zoo. If you don't plan to actually play with them it's enough to just stuff the toes with old newspapers and sew or glue on the eyes. Ears can be made by stuffing two points and securing them with elastic bands. Eyes, nose, mouth and ears can be embroidered on, working with buttons or coloured paper.

But it is much more fun if you can play with 'live' animals. You need your arm and hand, fingers and a little know-how.

The wicked snake

You only need eyes for the snake. Your thumb forms the lower jaw, the four fingers the nose. Pinch in a little of the sock fabric and your snake is ready. Let it wriggle and slide around the table.

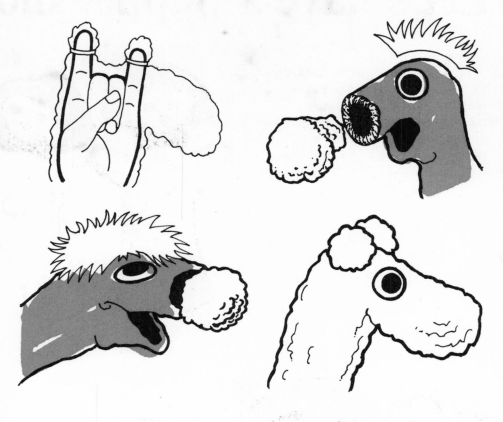

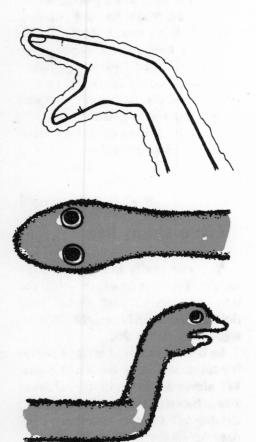

Snake language

Pull the sock up your arm and place your elbow on the table. Depending how you move your hand and fingers the snake is affectionate, naughty, bashful or cheeky; it may be a chatter-box or very quiet and shy.

Above, you can see how you can make the animal's head more flexible. Here it is your fingers which become ears that move by tying elastic bands around folds of fabric which aren't stuffed but filled with two fingertips.

The long nose is stuffed with crumpled paper. A pair of eyes are stuck on, and pulled over your other arm. Your second animal can have a fight with your snake, or perhaps they will fall in love with each other, who knows?

Your thumb and index finger can also be used to form the head, and the nose will become even more flexible.

Or you could open the end and glue in a nose made from different material. And don't forget hair made from wool.

Now paint on a mouth (red) on the lower jaw at the front and you have a lovely, ugly monster.

A few more suggestions

Tiny balls of wool become sweet little faces when stuck on your finger tips. Don't wind the wool too tightly.

You can have five puppets playing at once.

Place four faces on your left hand, these are the spectators or pursuers.

The fifth face on the right hand represents the 'star'. He talks to the audience. Or he is running away from his followers.

The one with the big mouth

Now we come to making a cardboard box monster. For this you need a biscuit box or a small shoe box, two ping-pong balls, a thimble, two strips of card and two pieces of material as long as your arm.

Glue the cardboard box together at the back so that it is quite secure. Now stick on a longer piece of card to the lid and a shorter piece to the bottom in such a way that your four fingers will fit in the upper strip and your thumb in the lower.

Now glue the fabric to the lid as well as the box and glue the edges of the fabric together.

Paint big black spots on the ping-pong balls and stick them on as eyes and the thimble as the nose. Paint the inside of the box a bright colour and your monster is finished.

Punch and Judy

You can make puppets for your Punch and Judy show from artificial clay and fabric. Shape the heads from clay (with a space for your middle and index finger inside) and paint them as you like. You could use tennis balls for the heads, or balls of polystyrene.

Your thumb on one side and your ring and little finger on the other make the arms of your puppet. Make a dress for it that will cover your arm up to the elbow. Cut two pieces of fabric in the shape of a dress and sew them together (see Sewing). Glue the dress to the head.

See the chapter on theatre to find out how to move your puppets.

Puppets on a string

Puppets on a string are puppets which are joined by the head and limbs to a wooden cross with wire or thread. This wooden cross can steer the movements of the various limbs. These puppets, therefore, are movable. It is a little difficult to build them — but it is a real art to bring them to life. Try it; when you present your own puppet show your audience will really admire your work. What you need is newspaper and wallpaper paste, medium wire and a pair of pliers, thin thread, wood, paints, scraps of fabric and felt.

The method: First bend the wire

into shape. Then tear the newspaper into shreds, prepare the wallpaper paste, dip the shreds in it and form the part with the damp lump.

Each part must have an outward pointing hook (uncovered). These serve to join the limbs to the body and eyes, through which to thread the string.

On the drawing we show the wire as a black line and the body parts with a broken line. If you follow these instructions nothing should go wrong.

The head
Add the papier-mâché mixture layer by layer and press it together.

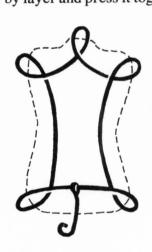

The trunk
The hook must protrude from the bottom of the trunk.

The upper arms
The loops within the arms help to form the papier-mâché shape.

The lower arms and fists

The thighs

The lower legs and feet

Now hook the various body parts together and close the open loops with pliers. Paint the body and varnish the surface.

Now build the wooden cross according to the drawing and fasten the various strings to it. Finally dress your puppet.

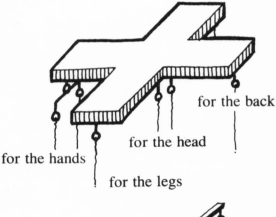

for the back

for the head

for the hands

for the legs

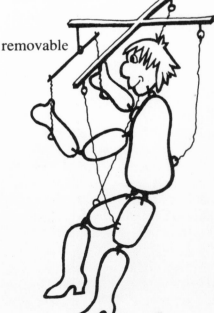

removable

126

All kinds of masks

There are many occasions where we come across masks nowadays. During a carnival many people put on masks, with colourful or funny faces. But robbers, too, use masks to disguise themselves. There are protective masks for dangerous work, working with a blow torch for example.

But a long time ago masks had a very different purpose. People weren't as knowledgeable as they are today and they didn't understand nature as well. They lived in fear of natural dangers and catastrophes.

To them the forces of nature were powerful gods. Thunder and lightning were wicked gods; rain, a bringer of fertility, and the sun, the source of warmth and light, were good gods.

Certain people within the community were chosen to deal with the gods, to communicate with them and perform rituals to seek their favour. Occasionally they offered sacrifices to appease them. An example is the medicine man among the American Indians.

Masks played an important part in these rituals. The people would hide behind their masks, or to communicate with a particular god would wear a mask which represented him.

Masks figure in the history of almost every human culture, from remote jungle tribes to our own ancestors, the Anglo-Saxons.

127

Eye masks

Eye masks are the simplest form of mask as only the eyes are covered. From cardboard, cut out a spectacle-like shape with broad rims, make two holes in the sides and thread through an elastic band. Now you can slip on the mask — and nobody will recognise you in a hurry! You can cut the eye masks in more sophisticated shapes, like our star mask.

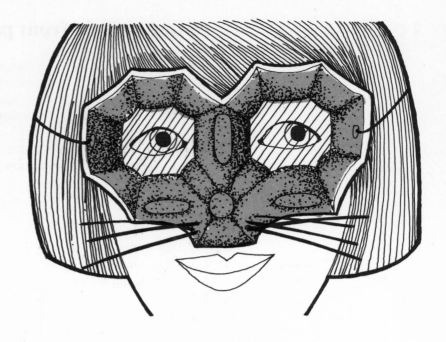

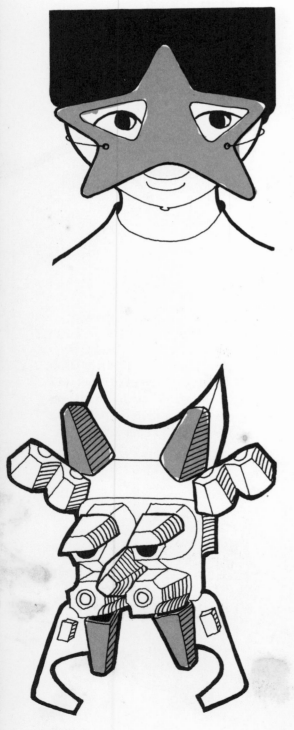

Egg boxes

Egg boxes are super for making unusual masks. Don't use the plastic ones, though, but those made from cardboard.

Because of their depressions and projections the cut up egg cartons need very little work to turn them into masks. Cut off the first two cups and the closure, paint it and you have your mask. It will stick to your nose almost by itself. Just cut out eye holes in the cups.

The cardboard material of the egg boxes can be cut very easily — and it is very light and comfortable to wear.

A dragon mask is a little more difficult to make, but still not too complicated. You need four cups, two lids and three pointed pyramids which you cut from the sides of the egg box (see drawing). The upper two cups are for eyes, but only cut half holes in them. The lower cups are for the upper lip to which you glue the pyramid teeth. Two of them you stick down there and the other two at an angle above the eyes. Paint it and it will look very impressive.

Other monsters

Here you can let loose your imagination. You can make many masks from egg boxes which are quite a horrible sight. You could make a nasty bird or a devil with horns. You could make beards and crowns. From the pyramid pieces you can make teeth and pointed tongues. The other important aspect, apart from the special shape of the egg box, is the material they are made from can easily be painted with poster paints and similar.

Depending how you apply the paint you could make a sad clown face or a sneering monster. You could make a whole family of monsters as these masks are fairly quick to make.

Masks made from papier-mâché

You don't need a lot of special equipment for face masks: newspaper, Plasticine, sticky tape, wallpaper paste and aluminium foil.

To begin with you prepare a mould. Form a face from newspaper; the nose is just stuck on. Then cover the mould with aluminium foil.

Smooth the foil down firmly so the shape of the face is quite clear.

Now tear off pieces of newspaper and soak them in the paste. Lay them over the mould. Continue covering the form with newspaper strips until the layer is about 5mm thick. Then leave the whole thing to dry. Ease the mask off the mould. Cut holes and slits for the eyes and mouth. Then paint your mask. One advantage with this method is that you can make as many masks as you like from the same mould; but you can paint them all differently so that you have a whole series of face masks. There are many ways to improve their appearance. You can stick on a beard and hair from wool, or even bushy eyebrows.

Finally, you only need an elastic band to hold the mask onto your face.

Face painting

Painting your face is fun. You can do it for a circus or theatre performance – or simply because you like to.

Two things are very important. Because you might smudge and smear a lot when painting your face, make sure your clothes are well protected. Secondly, you must cover your face with a protective cream before you use make-up on it as it can be harmful to the skin. You can paint your face with lipstick, eyebrow pencil and other things your mother may lend you, but do ask her first or you might be in trouble. But you can also buy special face paints. They come in many different colours.

Don't forget to remove the paint from your face afterwards. First wipe off most of it with cotton wool, then with cleanser or skin tonic and finally with soap and water. And you should put some moisturising cream on afterwards.

Tummy face with top hat

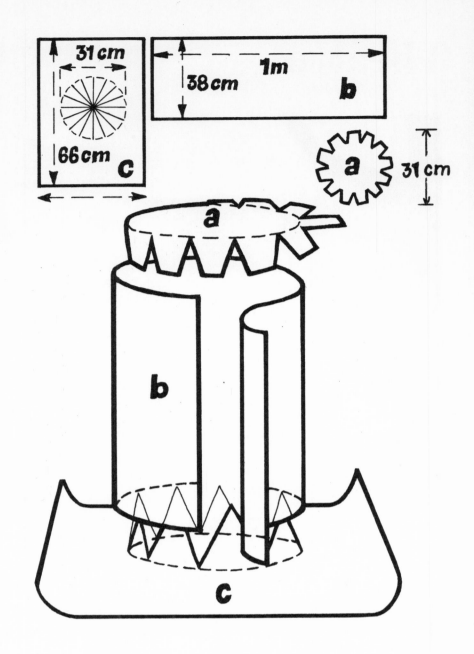

The tummy face with the top hat never fails as an attraction at parties, the circus or fancy dress party. School and village fêtes, too, are ideal venues for a tummy face, but the weather must be reasonably warm as you might easily catch a cold. So do it in the summer!

The first stage is painting the tummy. Again you can use your imagination, there are no fixed rules. Just a few tips: the navel would, of course, make an excellent mouth rounded in surprise. And the eyes are best situated on the nipples otherwise you have two elements not in keeping with the face. And in

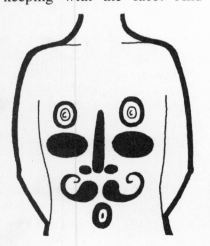

addition it is an advantage that they protrude a little anyway!

Now you have to build the 'top hat'. It must be very large so that your arms held over your head can fit comfortably, and have two small holes so you can see where you are going. You can find a drawing with the instructions to make the hat above. You need light corrugated cardboard and all-purpose glue as well as a pair of scissors. Nothing else.

Once your top hat is finished the fun can begin. Arrange a jacket around your hips so it dangles almost to the ground. And you'll be the funniest figure anyone has seen for a long time!

Fancy dress

Masks can be made from almost anything you come across. A wide sock, with eye holes cut out will disguise you completely. If you pull a nylon stocking over your head it will flatten your face totally altering and disguising your appearance.

You can dress yourself up (as described in the chapter about agents) with different hair, false beards, sunglasses, hats and scarves, then nobody will recognise you.

How to have fun with your fancy dress is described in the chapter about theatre. Why don't you have a fancy dress party and give prizes for the most original entrant?

Theatre

As long as there are people there will be theatre. Why is that? Because theatre makes it possible to express things that would be difficult to say otherwise.

Theatre, therefore, presents a good means of conveying information. If, for example, a theatre troupe from Greece performs a play from their homeland we receive quite a lot of information: about the country, the people, history, problems, festivals and sad events.

Although, through plays, it is possible to bring attention to injustices and try to bring about some change.

Theatre is art, and it expresses all aspects of our lives: humour, tragedy, love and conflict. And it brings us a great deal of pleasure!

You can just start to playact, by pretending to be someone you always wanted to be. You can in-corporate situations into the play which will involve other people.

The troupe

It is not that easy to perform theatre on your own. So find some other children who fancy having a go at it.

The parts

Think about what you want to perform and write a script. Distribute the various parts. Think about any costumes you'll need, where you want to perform and how you can attract an audience.

The rehearsals

You have to learn your parts but you can always leave a little to chance and your imagination, just make sure all the actors know the main story of the play.

The performance

When you come to performing your play it is better if you appoint one of you as the 'director'. He decides when you come onto the stage, where you should stand, and 'prompts' you if you forget your lines. And afterwards you should discuss your play with the audience. Did they understand it? Could it be made easier to understand? Should anything be changed to improve the play? What ideas do they have for a play? Invite them to take part and perhaps you will soon start planning another play.

Circus

For your children's circus you can make use of almost anything from this book: masks, puppets, magic and many other ideas. Make the costumes yourself, dress up as animals (wild beasts to be handled by a tamer), be your own acrobats and jugglers, but don't forget the clowns. Clowns are the most important part of any circus.

Clowns can make a part in a funny way. For example, if some of you are forever struggling on your pocket money if you make jokes about it your parents will soon know what you are writing about!

If you can play a musical instrument make some circus music.

Cowboy party

On the pages about 'masks and puppets' you will find many things that are also applicable to the theatre. But there is much more. If you really fancy playing at cowboys and Indians why don't you arrange a special party?

Invite your friends and tell them that they must come in fancy dress, dressed up as cowboys and Indians. And you can prepare a little surprise by performing a play. Find out all about how it really was with the red Indians and the white man. You can perform a small play showing that the Indians weren't the 'baddies' — but the white man who stole the red Indians' land. That will lead to discussion . . .

About children's and

The adults, too, have got the message! There are more and more theatre groups appearing who write plays specially geared to children and young people. They often tour the country with their plays, performing anywhere they can and are allowed to.

There are plays about the difficulties some children had when they tried to install an adventure playground in their town. There are plays about the problems between children and their parents, their teachers, problems at school or with the neighbours. Plays about love, work and unemployment, about

youth theatre

alcoholism, drug-taking and smoking. All these plays try to explain where the children's problems came from, whether it has something to do with their parents or what else the cause could be.

If there is a performance by such a theatre group near you why don't you go and watch it. Not only can you learn something (everybody is telling you that!) but the playwrights and actors, too, can learn from you. As they are adults they don't always know about your problems, anyway. So talk to them and tell them what is important to you.

Fancy dress party

Now you have made all those masks, big ones and small ones, face and tummy masks, funny ones and gruesome ones. Why should they lie forgotten in your rooms? Why don't you invite everybody to an open-air fancy-dress party (or in bad weather in the school or village hall).

Then you can produce a fancy dress fashion show. The compere explains how and why a particular costume was made. And the best ones get a prize.

Shadow play

Shadow play also makes a good performance. Just hang a white sheet between two posts and position a strong light on the back of it. Now you can perform a play behind the sheet, either written by yourself or from a book. The audience on the other side of the sheet will only see your shadows. You can use your hands a lot or work with large masks which aren't specially painted.

The faces of the players are not that important in a shadow play as they are not seen. The way you move your bodies and your gestures (jiggling your hands and feet about) are important. It is fun as you will soon find out . . .

Puppeteering

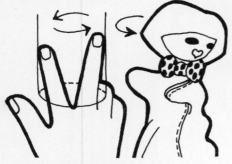

How do you move puppets during a performance? Here are a few tips:

Index and middle fingers pointing upwards and thumb and ring and little fingers form the arms. That's how the puppet is held.

Bend the thumb and ring and index fingers, the puppet stands in a normal position.

Bowing, carrying and turning the head.

The puppet stage

To build a stage you need four chairs, four posts and two blankets or sheets. Tie the posts to four chairlegs and fasten a blanket to them. One blanket reaches down to the floor, the other ends by the chair seats. You stand between them and perform with the puppets. Have a good look at the illustrations.

Stage for string puppets

Use the same principle here. Just push the chairs closer together and hang the sheets in reverse order. The one in front must leave enough space from the floor that the puppets can be seen in between. You stand behind the second sheet.

Stage set

Depending on what type of play you have written you can design a special 'set' for the stage. That is the background before which your puppets perform. Don't make it too complicated. A simply painted landscape and one or two houses with a road is enough for a city scene. A room, too, should be well but simply designed. It could look like the illustration above, behind the curtain. If you assemble there, in order, all the accessories you need you can always find everything at the right time. That should give you some ideas.

Magic and Tricks

Magic
Betting
Card Tricks
Coin Tricks
Experiments

Abracadabra

Magic — you must have heard that word many times, when there wasn't a magician to be seen anywhere. People describe things as 'magic' that are so beautiful and exciting one can hardly believe them.

And the word is true, too. Because one cannot believe the tricks a magician can perform. Here we want to unravel some of the mysteries of those good old

you can perform them with your eyes shut. If you have to interrupt your act because you have thought of something you've forgotten, or if at the height of tension an egg drops out of your sleeve, it does tend to destroy the magical atmosphere you have created.

If you should really have such a mishap there is only one thing to do: pretend it was all part of the act. Make a few mysterious movements with your hands and mumble a few secret words . . .

tricksters — just enough for you to get interested in the art and involved with 'magic'.

There are three important things in the life of a magician: his costume, his play-acting and his dexterity.

You will, of course, be much more impressive if you wear a top hat and dinner jacket or black robe. These help to create the right atmosphere.

More important is your ability to act. You will have that, don't worry. You must behave in a secretive manner, never disclose a trick, give yourself a mysterious name and behave as if you were the biggest magician in the world: arrogant, but friendly and inscrutable.

All there is to say about dexterity is that you must practice your tricks and the magic art until

The Ring and . . .

Applause, excitement — the great magician appears. With dignified gestures he speaks: 'Venerable audience, ladies and gentlemen! No other than the great Ali Baba himself bequeathed me the most mysterious ring in the world.

I have it here on the tip of my index finger so you can all see the mystery of its disappearance.

I hold out my hand and say the magic words which Ali Baba has taught me: 'Thingering — fingering — disappear my magic thing.'

I close my hand — and open it again — the ring has disappeared. Where is it? In my hand? No, it isn't. Look, it is empty.'

1. What you need for this trick is a strong elastic band, a safety pin and a ring. And now you make your secret preparations.

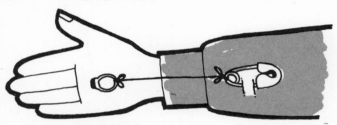

2. Tie one end of the elastic to the ring, the other to the safety pin. Try and make the knots as strong as possible, they must not come undone.

3. Fasten the safety pin to your shirt sleeve and pull your jacket or cloak over it. Now place the ring to the tip of your index finger.

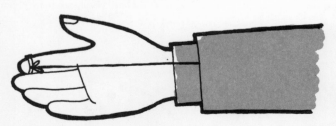

4. You always show the back of your hand to the audience, never the front. Then you fold your hand, and the ring disappears up your sleeve. Now you can show the whole hand.

. . . the talking box

'On the table in front of me are three boxes. One of them can talk, although you, venerable audience, will only be able to perceive a rattle. Which is the rattling box. I will let it speak, there . . . Remember which box it was. All right? Come forward and try to find the talking box. Can't you find it?'

1. Get four boxes, they could be matchboxes or similar — but you should paint them. You also need two buttons and a wide elastic band.

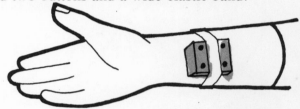

2. Place the buttons in one of the boxes and fasten it to your arm with the elastic band. Now cover it with your cloak or you'll be found out.

3. Now you must completely confuse your audience. If you pick up one of the boxes with your prepared arm it will rattle. If you use your other hand it will be silent.

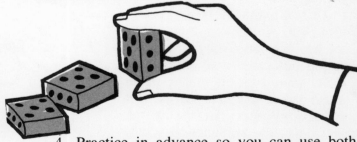

4. Practice in advance so you can use both hands equally well. Then rattle one box and let the audience look for it. Poor people!

The importance of balance

Now show your audience how you can balance all sorts of different things. You are assured of rousing applause – if you can really master the tricks. So you will have to practice a bit:

1. Fasten a thin thread or nylon string to a rope. Hold both in your hands and stretch them across. Now let a ping-pong ball dance on them. You have to practice putting it on – to take it off just throw it in the air and catch it with your hand.

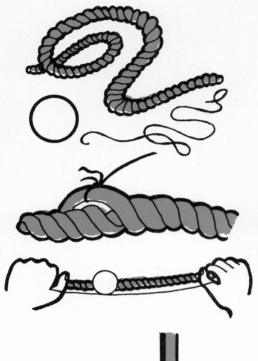

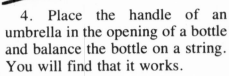

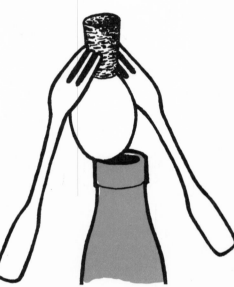

4. Place the handle of an umbrella in the opening of a bottle and balance the bottle on a string. You will find that it works.

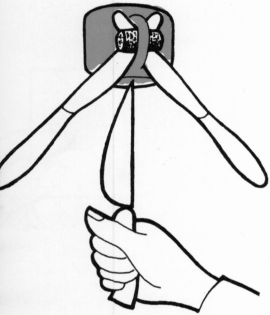

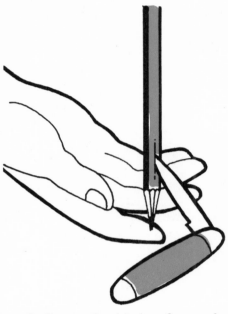

2. Fasten a cork to the handle of a cup in such a way that it will hold two crossed knives (see illustration). Now balance the cup on the tip of a knife. It is much easier than it looks.

3. Insert the blade of a pocket knife into a pencil and fold down the handle. Now you can balance the pencil on your fingertip because of the equal distribution of weight.

5. Who could balance an egg? You could – with the help of a cork in which you have stuck two forks. But you'd better practice in advance with a hardboiled egg.

Tricks with magnets

Electro-magnetism is quite a mysterious thing. If you blow some soap bubbles (made from warm water, soap and sugar!) and then comb your hair. Bring the comb near the bubbles and you'll see they will dance on the comb – because it is now electrically charged. Cut out a paper cross and fold it as in the picture. Place it

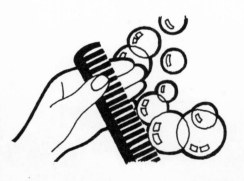

with its exact centre on the head of a pin pushed into a cork. Cover it with a glass (carefully). If you rub the glass with a cloth the point of the cross will move towards it.

The mysterious picture

You can use your newly acquired knowledge of magnetism for the mysterious picture, too. Show your audience a plate of glass; the glass of a picture frame will do. Let everybody look through the glass — there is nothing on it.

Now lay the glass across two books separated by a space. Before the eyes of the audience you sprinkle some finely chopped bits of cork or just some pepper . . .

Now you rub the glass with your magic cloth — and the crumbs will attach themselves to the underside of the glass. This isn't really that clever. But now the great magician speaks, 'Abracadabra, three black cats,' and taps the glass with his magic wand. And a mysterious house appears on the glass. Applause!

Tips

You can produce many more tricks using the force of magnetism. You only have to experiment a little. Being a great magician you could start a little booklet where you note everything you can think of, or what you have seen somewhere else that surprised you. Afterwards you will surprise yourself with the contents of your magic book!

1. For your performance you need a plate of glass, two books, a paintbrush, a cork, crumbs or powder and a little glycerine.

2. Paint a picture on the glass with glycerine and the paintbrush. It doesn't need to be an elaborate one, a simple house or star or something similar.

3. Now you arrange the two books and sprinkle the crumbs or powder in the space between them. Finally lay the glass across the books.

4. Rub the glass with the cloth and the crumbs will attach themselves to the glass underneath. If you now tap the glass, the crumbs will stick only to the areas covered with glycerine and the picture becomes visible.

Ruler and cork

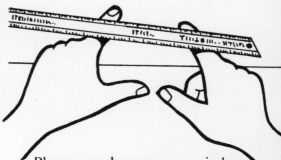

Place a ruler on your index fingers so that one end protrudes more than the other (see picture). Now move your fingers closer and closer together. To which side will the ruler fall? To neither. Your fingers will always meet in the middle of the ruler. Do you want to bet on it?

Cut a circle, a square and a triangle into a piece of paper. The circle and triangle must fit exactly inside the square, and the diameter of the circle must be the same as that of a cork. Now cut the cork as shown in the picture. If you have done it correctly the cork will fill all three holes completely.

Wax flowers

Did you know it's easy to produce wax flowers? Light different coloured candles and let the hot wax drip into a bowl of cold water. When the wax touches the water, the drips will form into flower shapes. Now stick the petals on thin, flexible wire sticks to make a nice, colourful flower. Try it out with different candles.

The magic belt

Ask three volunteers to the stage. Tell them you have some magic belts that enable one to look into the future. Explain to them that if each of them took one of the belts and hung it over themselves for a few seconds the belts would soak up all information needed to foretell the future.

Glue two or three sheets of newspaper together in such a way that you have one big sheet, about 150cm long. From it cut three strips each 8cm wide.

Glue the ends of the first strip together.

Twist one end of the second strip before glueing it to the other end.

Twist one end of the third strip twice before you glue it to the other.

Check again: the first strip has no twist, the second strip has one, and the third has two twists. If you hold them up they all look the same to the audience, don't they? Only you know that they are all different.

Now you ask each of the volunteers to walk in a circle three times while you say some magic words, perhaps like this:

'Turn once, turn twice, turn thrice — the belt will not tell lies!'

Now you take back each of the belts and cut them in half horizontally, as shown. Start with the ordinary belt.

When the second belt is cut up the result is one large ring, twice as big as the original. That means that fate will send the volunteer on a long journey round the world.

When you have cut open the first belt you will have two separate rings. You tell your volunteer that somebody is longing to meet him or her.

As everyone waits impatiently for the third belt you cut it open saying some magic words — and lo and behold you produce two narrow rings linked together. 'I suppose you don't have a steady girl/boy friend, do you?' you ask with a stern look on your face!

140

Betting is fun

The fact that some people have quite extraordinary hobbies is well-known. How fond of betting the British are will be talked about a little further on. Here's just a bet to begin with: I bet, for an ice cream, that you cannot stay underneath a table while I gently knock on it with my finger three times. I promise I won't bang hard, kick or rock it. Do you accept? Well, let's start. Under the table. Ready? I knock – once – twice . . . finish. Can you wait until tomorrow for the third knock? Get me my ice cream!

The betting British

It is quite incredible what the British will place bets on. Not just on horses, greyhounds or snails, no . . . And they don't just bet with how high an advantage the Labour Party will win the next election over the Conservatives. They also bet that Sugar Ray Leonard will win the fight against a Japanese, they bet that the first man on Mars is going to be Chinese, they bet that there won't be any snow at Christmas 1999. . . .

The same way that you can insure anything you can think of in Britain (starting with your life, to your nose, to your loss of hair) – the same way you can bet about anything that happens in the world. And because most British people are fond of sport most bets are usually fair play and not only for money. But one can also bet for money. It depends on whether you can afford the stake money you are challenged to put up for the bet.

If you are very thirsty . . .

If you are very thirsty make sure that all your friends have a full glass of Coke or lemonade before them. And then you offer your bet – but be clever about it, like this:

'I bet that I can drink up your glasses although I am standing about 2 metres away from the table – without a glass, hands or straw, or any other aid. And because there is a trick in it and I don't want to rob you of your pocket money, we will just bet for one penny.'

And who wouldn't join for just one penny! So you place a penny in front of each friend – and calmly drink up all the drinks. You lost the bet – but you certainly won't be thirsty any more!!!

Betting with dots

I bet that you can't circle 16 dots with one single line which only crosses itself once each time, and will produce a nice pattern as well. Well, let the others try it, it is not that easy. Draw the 16 dots in four rows of 4 dots, as shown below. If they have tried long enough, you show them.

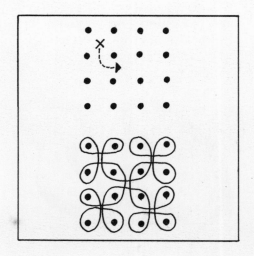

Betting and records

Betting and records have a lot in common. Most records are connected with a bet – doing something someone bet you couldn't. You could start to collect bets and records and you would soon have a book full of curiosities. Start with simpler things like:
- the longest river
- the deepest ocean
- the highest mountain
- the tallest human being
and anything else you think of.

Then you can start with real records. Some time ago a team of three men and one women staged a record in playing bridge. They played the card game for 210 hours without interruption. They should know it by now!

The fastest snail in the world belongs to a man in Indonesia. It has been given the name of 'Sanshapindo' which means something like 'old steamroller'. It is supposed to have travelled the length of the track of 10 metres in 11.3 seconds. But it apparently collapsed afterwards from exhaustion.

A tip: there is a book called 'The Guinness Book of Records' listing the craziest records: the largest tomato, the heaviest fish and many others. . . .

141

Nobody lives more dangerously tha

Springfield on a pale September evening. Two horses whinny before the 'Grand Canyon' saloon. A cat crosses the dusty cart track. Three dim lanterns shed a yellow light.

There is an icy silence inside the saloon. How long will the peace last? Simon Goose has been making money by the bushel all evening. And again the professional card player looks at his opponent with piercing eyes. He whispers '30 and 20 more. . . .'

The cowboy sitting at the other end of the table says quietly into the silence, 'I'll see you.' The Goose slowly lays the cards on the table, one by one: ace of spades, ace of hearts, ace of diamonds and . . . A sigh rustles through the assembled guests: Simon Goose adds the ace of clubs.

Then the cowboy stands up and pushes his chair away, 'Get up, you cheat. Where did you get the fifth ace?'

With two strides the cowboy reaches Simon Goose and pulls up his sleeve. There it is, a rubber sling. 'Well, well,' says the cowboy meaningfully. Then he raises his voice and says, 'You won't cheat again that quickly if I can help it. . . .' sweeps the money from the table and leaves the saloon.

Feel the card

Take a pack of cards and shuffle it well. Let someone choose a card. He should hand it to you in such a way that everybody else can see it but not you.

Take the card between thumb and index finger of one hand and 'feel' it with the other. You say 'Yes' and 'That could be it' and other clever words. Doing that you gently press together your fingers so you can just see the card on the bottom right, for example ten of clubs.

Well, they were rough times in the West. But nowadays, too, some people try to make money cheating at cards. The tricks are played especially while the cards are being shuffled. Don't get caught, friends. Be alert — and try your luck with a few tricks yourself. Then you will be able to see through the tricks of others more easily. . . .

Now don't call out 'ten of clubs' right away. Make it exciting and confuse your audience. Say, 'Must be a black card . . . could be a club, yes, it must be ten of clubs!'

the cheat . . .

In it together

You announce that you don't want to shuffle the cards yourself as you might be cheating. So a member of the audience selects a card. Your accomplice in the audience shuffles the cards and afterwards divides the pack of cards in two parts, to 'cut' it. Doing that he shows you the bottom card of one part without attracting attention. He then places the card selected by the audience on top of the unknown block and places the block with the card known to you on top.

You take the pack of cards and carefully, with a lot of contemplation, you look at each card. When you reach the card which was shown to you: the next one is the one you are looking for!

On your own

One clever-clogs in the audience accuses you of having an accomplice and challenges you to do it on your own. You reply that that would be quite a difficult task but being a great artist you would be able to do even that.

Carefully shuffle the cards, let someone select a card and separate the pack of cards in several smaller ones. With your thumb you gently lift up the upper card of one pack unobservedly. Now carry on like before. Place the stack with the card known to you on top of the card you are looking for. All clear?

Tricks on the eyes

If your audience isn't too knowledgeable about cards you can trick them with a little deception. From the pack of cards find the 7 of clubs and the 8 of spades.

You have the audience return these anywhere to the pack. Now you announce that you can find the cards with just one move. You speak a few secret words — and bang the cards on the table. How did you do that? Well, you have

placed the 7 of spades and the 8 of clubs on the top and bottom of the pile of cards and now pull them off in one stroke.

Only well versed card players will know that the 7 of clubs and the 8 of spades are not the same as the 8 of clubs and the 7 of spades. So, try it.

What a coincidence

Take two identical packs of cards, one for yourself and one for your partner. Now ask your friend to shuffle his cards, you do the same with yours — but unnoticed you look at the top card of your stack. Remember it well — otherwise the whole trick is lost. Do you know it?

Swap over the stacks. Your friend selects a card from your pack and you one of his. Place your selected card on the stack in front of you. Ask your partner to do the same. And remember: if your friend does exactly the same as you do, nothing can go wrong.

Swap the packs of cards once again. Ask your friend to find the card he had chosen from his stack — and lay it face down on the table. You find his card, too — as you know his card. It must be the one that is behind the one you remembered.

And now the great moment has come: your card is lying in front of

you face down. On a signal you both turn over your cards. And you won't believe the amazement of your audience: both cards are the same. Some will say it was a coincidence. So you repeat the whole exercise. And it works again!

Highway robbery

At the beginning of the last century some rather grim fellows roamed the countryside. Among them was a gang of rather nasty villains, a group that was always ready for another wicked trick. They lurked in the shadows to spring upon their victims — and played a wicked game with them.

'I will place thirty cards before you, you wretch. You must determine your fate yourself. If you select a card and I cannot find it immediately in the pack you are free to go. If I find it your last hour has come!'

The travellers had new hope — but the chief of the highway robbers never made a mistake. (He let the victims go free, anyway, once he had stripped them of their fortunes.) Do you want to know how his trick worked? All right, I will tell you the secret:

Take any 30 cards and place them in three rows of ten on the table face up as illustrated. Then ask someone to pick a card; but he must only tell you the row in which his card is. Re-stack the cards with this row of cards in the centre and the other two at the top and bottom of the pack.

Now play the cards out in the row again in such a way that the first card is on your left, the second in the middle and the third on the right. Then the fourth on the left again and so on to the end. Again you ask for the row of the chosen card. And you repeat the same procedure as before.

Now you again stack the cards with the selected row in the middle, and count them out until you reach 16. The sixteenth card is the one you are looking for, guaranteed!

You can do the same trick with 15 cards, too. Then, after taking up the cards three times, the card you are looking for is number 8.

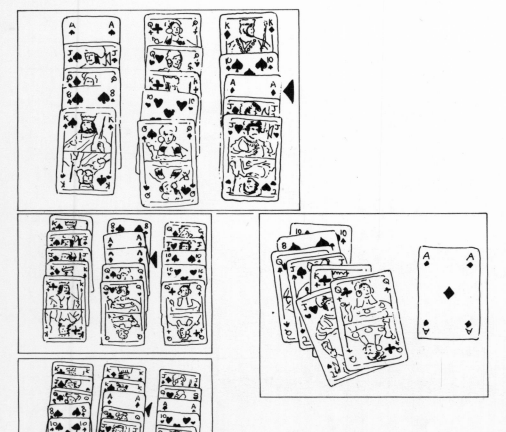

Let them dance . . .

This last card trick will turn ordinary ideas upside down. Whereas we normally expect things to break out of a certain order, this trick shows how the cards collect themselves from apparent disorder into an orderly file all by themselves.

Well, we say that we can put a number of completely jumbled up cards into the correct sequence just by spelling them out. Well, let's see . . .

We will show you a series of cards from 2 to ace which are not in order. It doesn't matter whether the series is of one colour or another.

We now say 'a' and place the first card on the table. Then say 'c'

The inseparable pair . . .

'Well, my friends,' you say and again place the pack of cards on the table. 'I will give you another nut to crack!'

Remove all the cards valued under 7 from a 52-pack leaving 32 cards, then lay the cards out in six piles of five cards each explaining as you go along. 'We now have two cards left. These are our inseparable pair. Who wants to try and separate them?'

'Nothing easier than that,' says Susan. 'What do I have to do?'

'Look at the cards and show them to the others. But not to me. And now place the cards each on one of the six heaps, it doesn't matter which, face down.'

Susan lays the cards on stack number three and number five. You pick up all the cards as illustrated, starting with stack number three, then two others, then number five, then two more. (That is, always put in first and fourth place the stacks on which the selected cards are laid.)

'I am now going to separate the cards into two stacks. Susan, you can choose one of them first.'

Susan chooses the one on the left. You deal the cards into two stacks, one left, one right, and so on. Then you say, 'You want the left one, don't you?' And you set aside the stack on the right. You must not make a mistake: you must always use the left stack. If Susan had chosen right you would have said, 'You want the one on the right?' and would still have set aside the stack on the right.

You must be clever about it — try to divert the attention of the audience by some clever talking. You always stay with your left stack, separating the cards and setting aside the one on the right. In the end you are left with two cards. Any guesses which ones?

Of course, they are always the ones chosen beforehand. Do you understand the trick?

and add the second card. Another card is 'e'. We say 'ace' and here is the right card.

Now spell 't', 'w', 'o' and each time place a card on the table. Then we say 'two' and there is the 2 next to the ace. We continue spelling out every card of the sequence until we have the king. And all the cards are in the correct sequence. (If the stack with the unused cards is finished, turn it round and start again.)

The whole point of the exercise is that we did, of course, put the cards in a certain order beforehand after all — although they appear to the audience quite disordered.

You have to place the 13 cards in the following sequence: 3 - 8 - 7 - A - Q - 6 - 4 - 2 - J - K - 10 - 9 - 5 - 3.

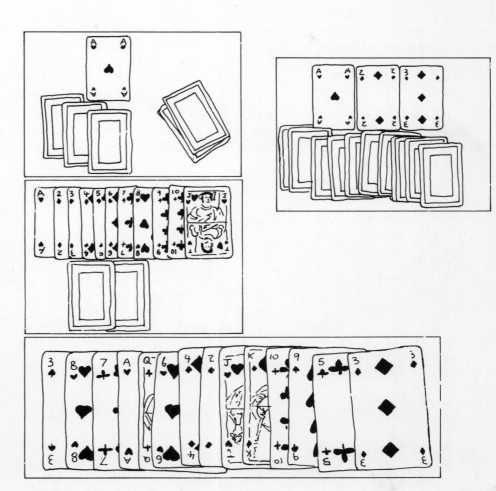

Making money with your hands

Once you have read through the next four pages you'll be surprised by the money-making tricks at your fingertips. When you've learned the coin tricks described here you'll become a proper money mint – at least that's how it will appear to your audience!

First things first, though. You have to practice very hard until you have complete control over the coins and it no longer seems as though they lead a life of their own. So, when you step on the stage, you will be sure of success. Good luck!

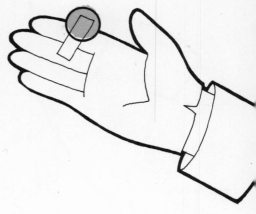

Coins everywhere . . .

Fasten a coin to the middle finger of your right hand with a piece of sticky tape in such a way that the coin's greater part is protruding over the index finger. It is now very easy to either make the coin fall back with an unnoticable little push of the index finger, or to make it stand up by using your thumb. You can see it more clearly on the illustrations here.

The sleeping 5p

Well, let's begin. The first lesson in playing tricks with coins is the 'sleeping 5p' – for experts this is just a warm-up exercise.

Take a pin and hold it between the knuckles of your index and middle fingers. Try a few 'dry-runs'. The pin must be held so tightly that it is completely hidden between your fingers when you bend them. Can you do it?

Now ask someone in the audience to give you a 5p piece and explain that it is a very tired coin (is the owner tired as well?). Meanwhile, you have opened and shut your hands several times so everybody knows they are

completely empty. Now you prop the 5p against the pin and open up your hand.

'It is still quite awake, this coin,' you say, 'but I can feel it getting tired.' And you slightly release the pin. And the coin falls flat and 'goes to sleep'.

'Is it going to wake up again?' you ask slyly. Then, with your free hand, you rub beneath the other and explain that you had to warm up the shilling a little. Unnoticed you straighten the pin – and lo and behold, the coin wakes up! Put it to sleep again and return it to its owner. Show your empty hands again . . .

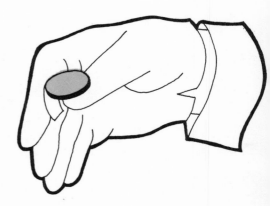

And now you have your coin factory. Push the coin up and take it away with your free hand (let it fall down, that is). Then you put it in your pocket (that is what your audiece will think anyway). Or you can find coins in the audience – in the ears, collars, on the backs of the people. Increase your speed, until the non-existent rain of coins is pouring down to tumultuous applause! But make sure you fasten the coin securely to your finger. It could fall off. . . .

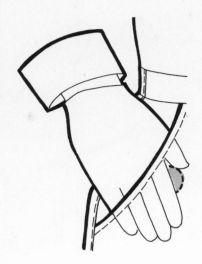

Where has the money gone?

Now here is another test. Let's see whether you pass or fail.

On the inside of your hand there are some creases. They usually form an 'M'. Place the coin exactly in the centre of the M. Turn over your hand. The coin will fall to the floor.

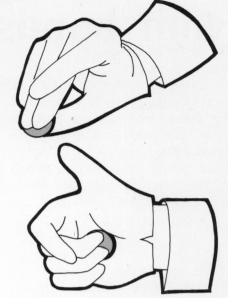

This trick can also be begun in a different way. Tell your audience you have an unexhaustible supply of money in your pocket. But that it is only available to you.

Take the coin out of your pocket. Put your hand in your pocket — and lift your hand while flicking up the coin. You pretend to take the coin away with your other hand and put it in your other pocket.

You repeat this several times. Then you say that your pocket was empty for other people. You prove it by flicking over your coin again and turning out your pocket. Great applause for the great magician!

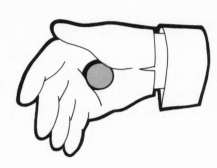

Place the coin again in the palm of your hand — and carefully bend the hand a little. Now you turn over your hand again. If the coin falls down again you have to practice a little more. Or try to change the coin for a smaller or larger one.

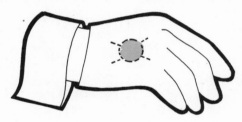

Try until you can really hold the coin in the folds of your hand without anyone noticing. You must make a lot of movements with your hands while you are talking but always keep both hands slightly bent. Then it won't be so obvious.

Now try to loosen the coin a little so that it rests on the upper parts of the middle and index fingers. And then do the same in reverse. Place the coin on both fingertips and press it against the folds of your palm. Let it go. If it doesn't stay, don't lose confidence, just practice a little more. Or do you seriously believe the great magicians of this world learned their trade in ten minutes?

Coins might fly!

As you should by now be able to do the trick with the hidden coin in your sleep we can make it a little harder.

For the 'flying coins' trick you need seven coins of the same size — the one you are most comfortable with. In addition you need a pair of gloves. Place six of the coins on the table, the seventh remains hidden in the palm of your hand, inside the glove.

left hand, three in your right, of which you quickly stick one in your fist. Now you tell the audience the coins could fly and hint at that with movements of your

hands. Then, with a loud 'abracadabra' you place the coins on the table. And look — from your left hand emerge four coins and two from your right. They can really fly!

Now continue until all your coins (6) have 'flown' from the right hand into the left hand. At the end you quickly release the seventh coin.

If you can manage this you can do all sorts of different tricks on the same theme. Let one coin dis-appear, produce another one and do the same with it (of course, it is always the same coin which you move from one hand to the other). But watch out for one thing: there must be nobody standing behind you as he would see the hidden coin!

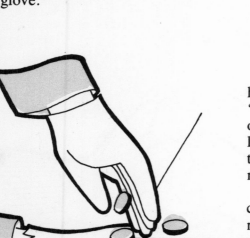

Now you tell the audience that your coins were trained to perform tricks. Divert their attention by talking and pull the coin out of the glove and keep it in your fist.

Now you count out three coins into each hand but let the hidden coin fall into the left, not the trick-hand.

Now you have four coins in your

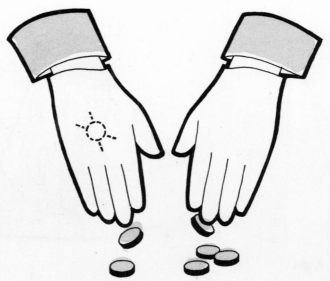

148

From 1 make 20

Now we come to the last of our coin tricks. After this you should be able to devise your own.

'From 1 make 20' is a trick that never ceases to amaze the audience as you will see for yourself. It goes as follows:

Place two 10p pieces, one 20p, two 5p pieces and a 1p piece on the table. Then you rub your head and say, 'Oh, I only need three coins for this trick, both the 10p pieces and the 1p. I can put the others away.' And you put the 5p pieces and the 20p in your pocket.

That's what your audience believes. You hold the 20p in your hand as practiced.

Now you place the two 10p pieces and the 1p in your other hand and show them to the audience. But very carefully push the 1p underneath the second 10p piece as shown in figure 3.

Now you ask for a volunteer and show him the coins again and say, 'You will be amazed,' and you push the 1p underneath the 10p piece.

Now you show the audience the hand with the two 10p pieces and at the same time slide the 20p in your other hand into your fingers.

Everybody in the room will be convinced that you have the 1p in your hand, your volunteer as well. You quickly press the 20p in his hand and tell him to close his hand very tightly. Press very hard! And he presses and presses . . .

Now the moment has come. 'Stop,' you say, turning towards the audience, 'this person has converted a 1p into 20p by magic. Can you believe it?' Of course, nobody will. So you tell your friend to open his hand. He finds — 20p. Careful, some volunteers have fainted when they've seen that!

Now we are at the end of our peep into the art of magic. If you practice a lot you could become a great magician. You can entertain your friends with these tricks and they will be impressed. So, work hard and good luck!

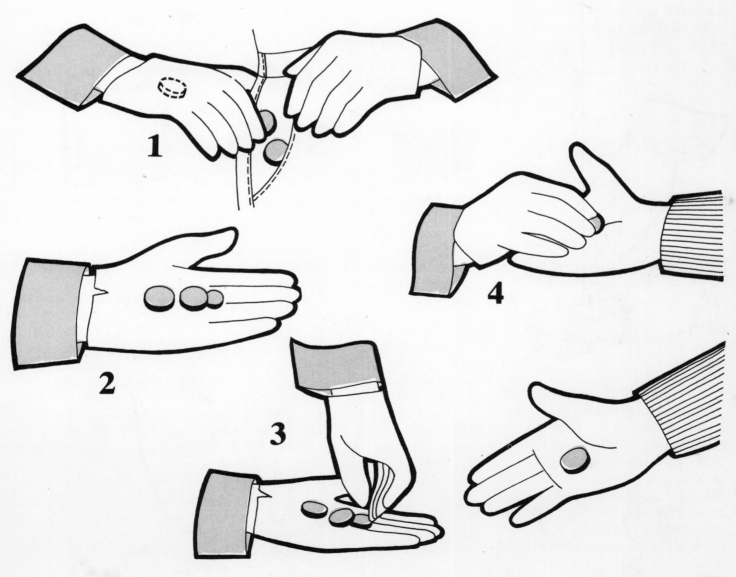

Experiment with experiments

Through experimentation scientists are always discovering new things. But it can be dangerous sometimes, too, as the rules of physics and chemistry cannot always be kept in check.

If you seriously want to try out scientific experiments you must be careful. Many people have been injured in this way. Never attempt anything without proper instructions, there are plenty of good books on the subject.

Here we deal with experiments more as a hobby. We want to show you some little tests with which you can surprise your friends. They are quite harmless but nevertheless very interesting — and good fun.

Not a knot

Take a long cigarette and wrap it in the cellophane of the outer packing. After twisting the ends you can make a knot in the cigarette. When you unwrap the cigarette again you will see that it is neither broken nor torn. The wrapping has distributed the pressure over the entire length of the cigarette. You only have to smooth it out a bit and it is as good as new.

That wicked coin

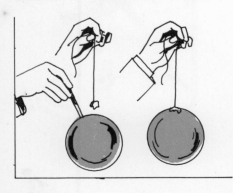

Playing with bubbles

Dissolve some soapflakes in warm water and add a little glycerine and brown sugar and you will have a super base to make bubbles. You can do a lot of things with bubbles.

Take two tubes (rolled from newspaper) and press the bubbles together. You can make them into many different shapes. You can prick them with a wetted needle. If you touch them with a scrap of paper on a string they will stick to it.

Try to blow two bubbles on top of each other and so make a chain.

Build a tower from six dice. Place a coin between the third and fourth dice. Can the coin be extracted from the tower without touching it — and without letting the upper dice fall down?

You can do it but you will need a ballpoint pen with a double pressing action. Hold the pen with the button to the coin and press on the clip. The button will shoot out and catapult the coin from the tower without it collapsing. (And you've won your bet!)

Metal that can swim

We all know that metal is heavier than water. If we throw a nail in the water it will sink. Well, let's see . . .

Fill a bowl with tap water. Place a paperclip, a razor blade and similar items on a piece of blotting paper and with the help of a fork gently lower it onto the surface of the water. When the paper has soaked up enough water it will sink to the bottom, but the objects will remain on the surface. The reason why? That has something to do with surface tension.

Ghostly rattle

Take a wineglass and fill it with dried peas. Now fill the glass to the rim with water and place it on the metal lid of a tin. The pile of peas will begin to expand, and you will hear a rattling that will go on for hours as the peas fall on the lid. They soak up the water and swell up: they pile up and flow over the rim.

Submerging games

Take a jam jar and fill it to the rim with tap water. Submerge some objects in the water. These could be a diver, a submarine made from a piece of orange peel, or a little bottle holding a glass tube filled with enough small beads to prevent it from sinking. (The bottle's cork should be pierced.)

Now seal the jar with waxed paper or cling film and an elastic band. If you press on the cling film the object will sink down deeper, if you release it, it will come up again.

It's all to do with 'uplift': the air contained in the orange peel is compressed and the uplift is reduced. Or the uplift of the little bottle decreases because water is pressed into the bottle. The air inside it is compressed.

151

Clever acrobat

Trace the little acrobat on the right twice on white paper and cut out both figures. Glue them together fixing a penny between each hand. Then paint your little acrobat.

He can perform clever tricks, he can balance on your finger or a rope. The reason is that you have moved his point of gravity downwards by inserting the pennies. The acrobat therefore always points his feet upwards.

Centrifugal force

Thread a piece of string through a narrow tube and tie a small weight to one end. Tie a larger weight at the other end.

Give this to a friend and ask him or her to make the small weight lift the larger one. When you have waited long enough for their feeble attempts, show them how it is done. Hold the tube upright and spin the small weight round and round in a circle. Support the large weight with one hand (see figure 1). The small weight will go into a larger and larger circle and will pull the large weight up (see figure 2).

It is the centrifugal force of the small weight spinning in a circle which causes the string to travel up the tube. As soon as you stop the spinning the large weight will drop down again.

Take care to use strong string and tie the weights very securely so that they do not fly off.

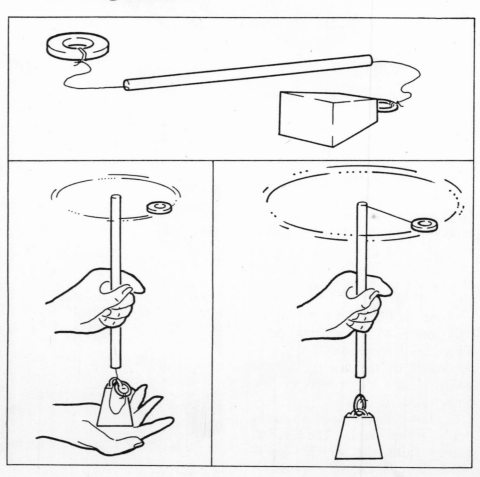

152

Balloons on the ceiling

Inflate some balloons and secure them with a knot. Then rub them for a while on a woollen jumper. If you now hold them against the ceiling they will stay there as if they were stuck.

This experiment has to do with electricity. Rubbing the balloons on the jumper causes friction which give them an electrical charge. They pick up minute negative particles from the wool. And they will stay on the ceiling until these particles are discharged to the ceiling. That can take quite a long time as the ceiling is a bad conductor.

Jet powered sardine tin

Secure an aluminium tablet tube inside an empty sardine tin. Fill the tube with a little water and pierce a hole in the end of it. Now place three short candle ends underneath the tube and light them.

Then immediately set the sardine tin on water in the bath and the sardine tin will steam along. The candles create enough heat to bring the water inside the tube to the boil. That results in steam which expands. It can only escape through a small hole in the tube. That creates a jet which propels your little boat forward.

The returning tin

Cut a slit into the centre of the bottom and lid of a round biscuit tin. Insert a piece of thick rubber band through the slits and fasten the ends with pins. Inside the tin you hang a weight from the middle of the rubber band with a paper clip.

Close the tin and roll it. The tin will return to its starting point where it will come to a stop. This is the result of the law of gravity which causes the weight to pull downwards as much as possible. The elastic has twisted itself as you've rolled the tin. The force of gravity pulls the weight downwards, and the elastic unwinds.

The force of air pressure

Another test that looks like a trick. Fill a glass with water three-quarters full. Cover it with a piece of waxed paper or a postcard and carefully turn it upside down. Now take your hand away – the paper will stay on the glass, no water escapes. The force of air pressure against the paper is a hundred times greater than the water pressure. Nothing is lost!

You can do the same test another way – and again amaze many people.

Place a thin wooden board over the edge of the table and cover it with a sheet of newspaper so that the long side of the paper is parallel to the edge of the table. Now with your knuckles knock a sharp blow on the protruding edge of the board – and it will break off. The air resting on the newspaper is holding the wood firmly to the table!

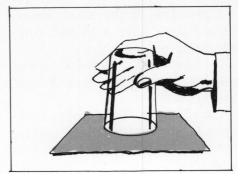
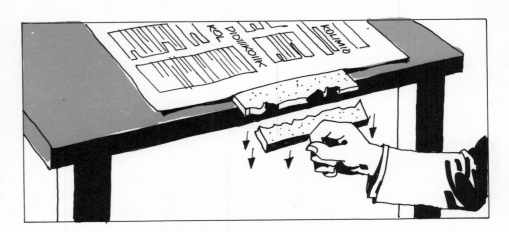

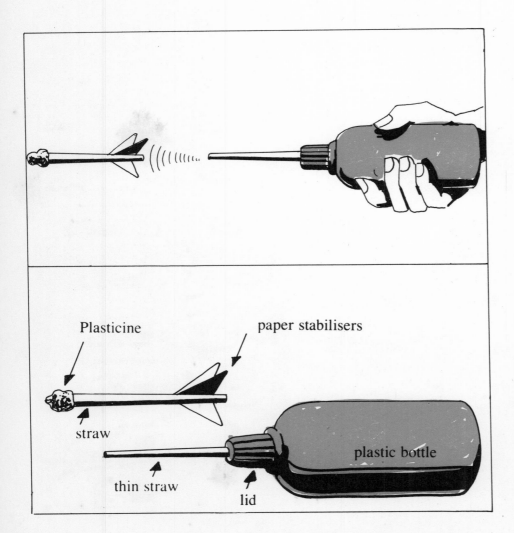

Plasticine

paper stabilisers

straw

thin straw

lid

plastic bottle

Which is stronger?

And now we are going to build an air pressure rocket. You will need an empty plastic bottle with a lid. Drill a hole in the lid and insert a thin straw in such a way that you can seal all the remaining space with glue. Glue three or four stabilisers from coloured paper to a fat straw, which will fit over the straw glued into the bottle. Form the point of the rocket from Plasticine. Fit the rocket over the straw and compress the bottle. The rocket will fly off!

And a tip: the firmer you fit the Plasticine-tipped rocket to the straw in the bottle, the more force is needed to 'blast off' the rocket and the faster it will go!

Let's make a mini movie show

Copy one of the five picture strips below, glue it to thin card and cut it out.

Now cut out the eight individual pictures complete with their numbered flaps.

Cut off about a third from a cork and make eight slits in it. Insert the pictures with their flaps in the cork in correct order. Cut out a 3cm space from the side wall of a cigar box and fold about 2cm inwards at a right angle.

Now make two holes in the centre of the lid and bottom of the box. Paint the entire inside of the box black.

You now need an old ballpoint refill which you bend as shown in the illustration.

Drill a hole through the centre of the cork. Insert the handle through the hole, first from the outside through the bottom of the box, then through the cork and then through the lid.

When you turn the handle clockwise and look through the viewer you can watch your mini movie!

When the handle is turned each picture is visible to the eye for only a brief moment before it is replaced by the next one. As your eye is slow you are still watching the first picture — although it has already disappeared. When you turn the

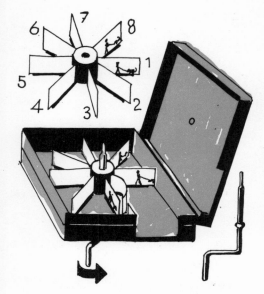

handle showing the individual pictures they melt into each other and appear to be moving.

And the great film studios work in just the same way as your mini movie. There, too, the film is separated into individual pictures which only start 'moving' when shown in quick succession.

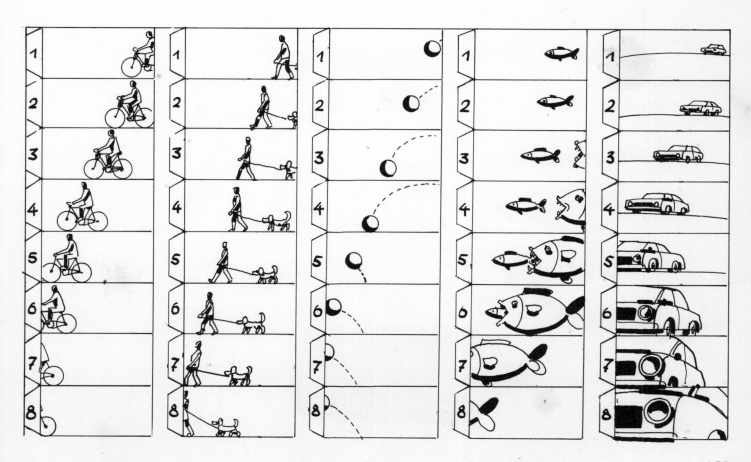

Index